"Our church has suppo[rted] since September 11, 2001. [M] lenges of the city through th[e] people. It's a powerful testim[ony of what God is doing in New] York City!"

— **Dr. Jack Graham**
    Pastor, Prestonwood Baptist Church
    President, Southern Baptist Convention

"Those who received a blessing from Taylor Field's earlier book, *A Church Called Graffiti*, will not want to miss this stirring narration about *Mercy Streets: Seeing Grace on the Streets of New York*. Here the reader will find the same remarkable blend of sensitivity to human suffering and deep insight into divine resources within the Scriptures."

— **Bruce M. Metzger**
    Professor of New Testament, Emeritus
    Princeton Theological Seminary

"Taylor Field includes us in his journey of discovering Christ's heart for the city. As you meet the men and women of *Mercy Streets*, you'll understand why Christ wept over the city. Your heart will be stirred to join Christ in taking His hope to those lost in today's urban jungles."

— **Bob Reccord**
    President, North American Mission Board

"Taylor's ministry among the homeless and impoverished is a challenge for all believers to follow Christ's call to serve even the least of those among us. What a story Taylor has to tell of grace and mercy!"

— **Zig Ziglar**
    Author, Motivational Teacher

MERCY STREETS

MERCY STREETS

SEEING GRACE
ON THE STREETS OF NEW YORK

TAYLOR FIELD

BROADMAN
& HOLMAN
PUBLISHERS

NASHVILLE, TENNESSEE

0-8054-2630-2

Published by Broadman & Holman Publishers
Nashville, Tennessee

Dewey Decimal Classification: 307.76
Subject Heading: CITY LIFE \ URBAN SOCIOLOGY
CITY MISSIONS—NEW YORK (CITY)

All pictures were taken from the walls and sidewalks
of Lower Manhattan.

1 2 3 4 5 6 7 8 9 10 07 06 05 04 03

For Him

Clear, tough-minded, practical, yearner,
Jesus the fierce one, the stark table-turner,
Jesus the gentle, the prodder, the poker,
Patient with fools, the dead-serious joker,
Teacher of Scripture, hero of whores,
Indifferent to money and feeder of scores.
Jesus the sad one who laughs and who cries
For people like me who are not so streetwise.
Jesus who looks beyond numbers to faces
Seeing some mercy in all the "wrong" places.
Jesus the mender, You take me apart,
Put my heart in my throat and my eyes in my heart.

I pray also that the eyes of your heart may be enlightened.
EPHESIANS 1:18 NIV

It was as if I were cured of color blindness.

— David Livingston, the famous missionary
in his explanation of accepting Christ at age twenty

Contents

Street Vision

Acknowledgments

I'M MORE FORTUNATE THAN anyone who ever won a jackpot. I am surrounded by people who care for others and who wish me well. Many thanks to my coworkers at Graffiti Community Ministries. Their love for others, especially since September 11, has been exceptional. The work of the hundreds of mission teams, who take the people of the city into their hearts, will never be fully recognized in this life. My deepest gratitude goes to our church and to the brave ones who consented to share their story. They are listed in the back of the book.

Both my editor, Gary Terashita, and my book agent, Bruce Barbour, have become friends whom I deeply respect. Their encouragement to me has been priceless. Without Zig Ziglar's help, the connections for writing this book would have never been made. Thank you.

The names of some of the people in this book have been changed. To protect privacy or to make a point, the circumstances of some of the characters have been modified. I am grateful to all these friends who helped me to see.

Many thanks to my two strong sons, Freeman and Owen, who have endured my strangeness and the apartment we chose to live in. Most of all, I thank Susan, my wife and soul mate, who has accompanied me every step of the journey and given wise counsel on and off the streets.

My Prayer

AS I FLEW FROM NEW YORK to Raleigh, North Carolina, I kept looking for patches of wilderness. I'd read for decades about the megalopolis, the vast string of cities and communities extending from Boston to Washington, D.C., that had almost completely merged together. And south of D.C., all I could see were houses and developments and roads. From my plane window, the whole eastern seaboard seemed like one vast city.

I have a string of books on my shelf that talk about the huge population shifts in the last hundred years, new paradigms of thinking about the world, fresh models for ministry in the city. I love those kinds of books. But this book will not be one of them.

For four decades and more, these books have been proclaiming that the explosive growth of cities around the world has caused a massive shift in humanity. By now, this has become obvious. Our planet is filled with cities.

The nineteenth-century dichotomy between nature and civilization is gone. Our cities affect the farthest wilderness. In the end, cities may be all we have. They are a part of nature, and the rest of nature that is adapting to it is thriving. There is pleasure in seeing Yosemite. Is there pleasure in seeing a parking lot?

The following pages of the book rest on Paul's prayer for us in Ephesians 1:18–19a: "I pray that the eyes of your heart may be enlightened so you may know what is the *hope* of His calling, what are the glorious *riches* of His inheritance among the saints, and what is the immeasurable greatness of His *power* to us who believe" (emphasis added). God gives us glasses to see the *hope* in the people He has chosen (chaps. 1–7). God helps us see the *riches* that are already ours as inheritors of the city surroundings (chaps. 8–14). He finally helps us see the *power* of His mending work even in the chronic and sudden traumas of the city (chaps. 15–21). As the entire letter to the Ephesians shows, God's healing action affects the cosmos, society, church, family, and individual, if we could only see it. No doubt boredom, indifference, addiction, and fear can walk the harsher streets of the city. But also mercy.

People are precious to God, so cities must be His treasure. This book is about seeing treasure. I'd love someone to toss the book aside and take a walk on the streets, seeking that treasure. In ten years the statistics will have changed, the paradigms will have shifted again, and the incidents written about here will have been forgotten. I don't want to share facts about the city; I want to share a love for the city. That is my prayer. Theories evolve, but opening our eyes to a love for the city is something that can last a lifetime and perhaps longer.

Beginning: Jesus

As He approached and saw the city, He wept over it.
LUKE 19:41

The question is, not what you look at,
but what you see.
HENRY DAVID THOREAU

HE DIDN'T GROW UP IN THE CITY. He didn't really speak like a city person. It seemed He would rather talk about the lilies of the fields than about the lines of a building. From this lack of experience, you might think He was naive about the city.

But not really.

He'd seen the city when He was twelve. He'd seen the swirl of activity and the crowds of people through the eyes of a boy. But these things didn't seem to distract Him, even then. Later, in the confusion of departing, His parents thought He was lost in the city.

But not really.

As a man, He cried for the people of the city. Stinging, burning tears and in front of the other guys. When we love something, we give it power to hurt us, and from the way He acted, He must have loved the city a lot.

When He walked on the streets of the city, He saw things that His friends did not see. They wrote about it later. At one place in the city, people who passed by saw simply a group of sick people. But Jesus stopped to talk to one man who seemed hopelessly sick to everyone else, the ones who were more "aware." The man had been sick for thirty-eight long years. The city accepted his perpetual illness. It had made a niche for him. But Jesus asked him the question that the others had been too streetwise to think of: "'Do you want to get well?'" (John 5:6). You might think that Jesus was just making conversation.

But not really.

At another time in the city, Jesus' friends looked at a man who couldn't see. They saw him as a starting point for an interesting and relevant theological discussion. But Jesus looked at the man in a different way, and He saw something else. He helped that hopelessly blind man to see, and through His action, He helped His disciples to see too (John 9:39). With that, you might expect that Jesus had done enough.

But not really.

Yes, Jesus knew the city—the crowds, the noise, the endless deals, the flow of money, the heat, the cynicism, the heartache. Somehow, He saw something in the people the city had written off, things no one else saw. To be streetwise means to know the ropes, to keep anyone from taking advantage of you, to be tough. Jesus showed us a deeper kind of street wisdom. Jesus walked the streets, and as He did, His companions walked with Him. They puzzled about what He did in the city at the time.

Jesus didn't grow up in the city. But He set His sights and headed toward the city with determination. In the end, as He expected, the city crushed Him.

But not really.

Prologue

WHAT AM I DOING ON THE STREET on this hot summer morning? Nothing much. Looking for a flophouse. Yes, a flophouse. A seedy, cheap, rundown hotel for vagrants and transients. There used to be a lot of them in midtown almost thirty years ago. I never go back there now. I don't know if the one I stayed in as a young fool is still there. But now that I am an old fool, I have set my face toward Times Square, and I am determined to find out.

A drop of perspiration slides down from my forehead and touches the top of my glasses. So much has happened to me since I was nineteen and first put my foot in Manhattan. Now every block brings back memories of individuals and objects. Every street reminds me of the changes that have happened in me. Like eye surgery, the people, buildings, and experiences have been the lasers that have shaped my sight. Some of the work on my "eyes" has been more uncomfortable than I had expected. In my mind's eye, I see the faded, dirty hotel, a needle in a haystack of buildings. On the outside I case the street like a detective; on the inside I wonder if the eye patches have come off yet.

You guessed it. I'm looking for more than just a flophouse. I'm not searching for a place to stay this time. I'm searching for a sign, a message on the wall, some little hint of what in the world God is doing in the city.

Do I find this wild, rickety flophouse? I'm not telling. You'll have to read the book to find out. But the following chapters tell what I remember.

Street Shades

(SEEING HOPE IN THE PEOPLE
GOD HAS CHOSEN)

CHAPTER 1

Vision:
New Jerusalem

"And the name of the city from that time on will be:
THE LORD IS THERE.*"*

EZEKIEL 48:35 NIV

In the cosmology of my dreams,
Manhattan is the New Jerusalem.

KATHLEEN NORRIS

THE LOCK HAD BEEN BLOWN off the door. There was still a little latch that kept the door from swinging wide open as I undressed and got in the bed. An old fan circulated the humid air. The squawks, honks, radio music, yells, and barks of all of Times Square wafted into my window. The dreary hallway outside creaked with many entrances and exits. I was nineteen years old; this was my first night in New York. I knew absolutely no one in the city. I didn't even know what the word *flophouse* meant, and I was sleeping in one.

I got there effortlessly, by simply stepping into the river of humanity flowing to Manhattan. I was on my way to school in Europe and had a two-day stopover in New York City. I don't think my parents realized what I was doing. As I got off the plane at JFK airport, I was clueless. At nineteen, planning ahead was not my strong point.

I had no idea what to do next. I drifted with the flow of people from the gate to the baggage claim area. The press of the crowd, the aggressiveness of the limo drivers trying to take my bags, the shouts of family greeting family on a hot summer day were invasive but not unpleasant. I drifted out to the baking sidewalk and breathed in the humid air, laced with carbon monoxide.

I saw a bus that had a sign that read "Times Square." I had heard of that place, although I had no idea what it was. I thought about the name. "Times"—was there a big clock there? "Square"—was it a park? Was it something mathematical—"Times Squared" maybe? Still, it was a familiar word in a sea of baffling information. I got on the bus. We lurched toward Times Square in heavy traffic. It took a lot longer than I expected. The skyline of Manhattan loomed ahead as the bus bounced from pothole to pothole. I felt I had landed on another planet. The height of wheat elevators in Oklahoma was nothing compared to this. The large cities I had seen before seemed like toys beside this. The buildings and towers ahead had the restrained power of a vast cluster of alien spaceships before liftoff, yet it was as gray and solemn as a graveyard or a penitentiary.

It was more than larger than life. It was mythical, stupendous, and in my nineteen-year-old heart as I held on to the back of the seat in front of me as if I were on a roller coaster, the New York skyline became etched in my hopes and my fears.

I got off at the bus station at Times Square. Still clueless. I walked up the street. What I saw was the Times Square that is gone now—rows of porn shops and peep shows, men standing outside trying to pull you in, teenage boys with cardboard boxes and shell games or card tricks trying to get you to watch, prostitutes in fishnet stockings and miniskirts. The streets themselves smelled like the old movie theater at home to which no one would go. The sidewalks were caked with gum and a film of grease. It was a little like walking along the midway of the state fair at home, except that the costumed assistants, bearded ladies, dwarfs, barkers, and pickpockets were all bumping into you and then perhaps looking right through you. Even the tenement buildings on the side streets, with their sagging structures and rusted fire escapes, seemed to have lost their innocence.

I paddled through the river of flesh, wearing my backpack, a gawking nineteen-year-old lad looking for a port. I was looking for a sign of safety, some sign of reassurance, a shelter from the carnival of humanity around me. I finally saw a sign, wedged between a faded circus poster and some graffiti: "Rooms—$10 a night." I glided into the old brick building with the broken windows. The lobby smelled like old gym clothes. "Could I have a room, please?" I squeaked. The man at the desk did not look at me but took my money and showed me my room. Only now can I speculate on the meaning of all the noises and footsteps that went on through the night in that place. I only know that on my first night in New York, I slept the sleep of an innocent idiot, and I was neither robbed nor harmed in that place of ill repute and broken dreams. Protection was there after all, even though all the signs were against it. I count it as the first of many miracles.

At age nineteen, I did not believe in God, but I loved nature and open spaces. Yet, I too was drawn into the whirlpool of people

5

called Manhattan. What drew me to the city in spite of myself? Since so many people profess to dislike city life, why do we humans continue to build cities? I cannot explain it. Neither can I explain why ants make anthills, bees make beehives, or beavers make beaver dams. Humans make cities, and in one sense, despite our protests, cities with their cars, pollution, and concrete are just as much a part of nature as beaver dams, beehives, and anthills.

Elie Wiesel once said that "God invented people because he loves stories."[1] It was the people that drew me to the city, and, I suppose, their stories. Sure, the city is a bonanza for stories about people, but I had a lot to learn about the streets.

CHAPTER 2

Being Invisible

The poor man and the oppressor have this in common:
The LORD gives sight to the eyes of both.

PROVERBS 29:13 NIV

Our point of view is determined by our
point of viewing.

PAUL MINEAR

7

HOW STRANGE THAT IN ORDER to learn how to see, we must remember what it is like not to be seen. When I left Times Square and finally arrived in Berlin, I thought I had the world by the nose. Sure, I was lonely, but attractions were everywhere—art museums, live music, movies. Movie theaters were on every corner, with movies the likes of which I had never seen before. Movies with plots I had never imagined came from all over the world to Berlin. As I blasted through the bowels of the earth in a subway, I felt as though I was quite the cosmopolitan international intellectual.

One night in December, I saw a very late movie, all alone, in downtown Berlin. I lived far away from the center of town, but my room was easy to get to by subway. I did not know that, at that time in Berlin, the subways closed completely at 1:00 A.M. Brilliant me. I stared at the iron grating of the subway at 1:30 A.M., in shock, and tried to figure out my next move. I couldn't walk. It was too far. I didn't have enough money for a taxi or a room. I had absolutely no family or friends anywhere in the area. I could think of nothing to do but wait in downtown Berlin for the subway to open.

I shivered and stood next to the iron grating for about ten minutes. That was totally boring and I was exhausted. I began wandering around the streets of Berlin, wondering what to do. The city was so cold and gray after midnight. Every door and window were shut. I felt lost and less like a cosmopolitan intellectual every minute. I realized that in a flash I had gone from a university student seeing a movie to another kind of person, a person with no resources—no money, no friends, no home. I roamed the empty streets, feeling like a criminal. For the first time in my life, I began to think a little bit like a street person. As I walked, I began to look furtively for a dark, safe place where I could hide and maybe go to sleep.

I tried to look casual as I wandered behind an apartment building, hoping that no one would call the police. I found a piece of ground in the back of the building that didn't look too hard. I

8

curled up in a fetal position, but my jacket wasn't large enough to warm me. I began to shiver. I buttoned my jacket and waited. After an eternity, I looked at my watch. Not even fifteen minutes had passed. I remember looking up at the few stars I could see in the cold sky. The night seemed like a prison. I got up and wandered the streets again, looking for some warm place to sleep. In my mind at that time, no God existed, so I tried to bolster my strength with what little philosophy I had. "Nietzsche says that anything that doesn't kill me, strengthens me," I told myself. The wind whipped under my jacket. I didn't feel very strengthened.

I drifted toward the train station in the center of town. To my great delight, it was open. I wandered the lobby area, looking for a place to lay down. I turned a corner, and I saw it, a little enclave, and there they were—people just like me. They were huddled together for warmth, homeless men and women, sleeping like children. To others it might look like a pretty ratty gaggle of lost souls, but to me it was beautiful—a warm place to slumber.

It doesn't take much to describe what a little exhaustion, a little cold, and a little disorientation can do to a twenty-year-old's sense of propriety. I didn't hesitate for a moment. I curled up next to the group and went to sleep instantly, like a squirrel that had finally found its nest.

The next thing I remember was a kick to the midsection. I woke to see huge police officers, big as linebackers, poking and kicking people to wake them up. From my perspective, with my head on the hard slate floor, they looked like giants. They used loud voices, as if they were awakening a bad dog. It was clear we couldn't sleep there. Wordlessly we each got up and shuffled off separately back into the night, a diaspora of helplessness.

I finally got through the night, but I learned something very important. The kicks did not hurt me. Not at all. What hurt me was being a thing, an object, a gunnysack of trash to be disposed of, worthy only of language fit for an animal, an invisible person. The authorities never looked me in the eye. That is what cut.

People often come to the city in order to be invisible. But in the end, it is a horrible thing to be invisible. On that night in Berlin, I told myself that I would never forget the small taste of cold, boredom, and human indifference. But I have.

In Deuteronomy, we are told to be kind because we remember what it is like to be in a tough situation. "Do not deprive foreigners and orphans of their rights; and do not take a widow's garment as security for a loan. Remember that you were slaves in Egypt and that the Lord your God set you free" (24:17–18 TEV). Lord, we remember.

We never know the whole story. It was only by not being seen that I began to see the people I normally look through each day. They drift through the public areas of a city. They look for a nook where they won't be a bother. Maybe they look for a little mercy. For me, remembering that hard moment was a plow that tore up my heart and made me open to seeing a little bit more of the street.

CHAPTER 3

Small Deeds

"Who despises the day of small things?"
ZECHARIAH 4:10A NIV

Great city, great loneliness.
LATIN PROVERB

11

WE TALK A LOT ABOUT GREAT DEEDS, I think, because we have a kind of collective amnesia about our personal lives. We simply don't think about or remember our own experience. There is a strange enchantment that deludes us into thinking it is only the big things that affect our lives. I remember reading once that the thing that makes a person go insane is not the great tragedies of life. It is the broken shoestring, when you are in a rush, and running out of time.

Just as it is not the big things that push us into a breakdown, it is not the grand programs that often bring us to God. It is the little moment, a look, a small act of undeserved kindness. I'm afraid that as we grow older, we delude ourselves into thinking that our big plans have made the difference. We forget.

I like to think, in my own mind, that one of the things that made Jesus so special was His ability to remember. As the story of Jesus' early life goes, an angel told Mary that she was pregnant by the Holy Spirit, and an angel told Joseph that Mary was pregnant by the Holy Spirit, but there's no evidence that angels told anyone else in their village about this wonderful experience. Even as a pastor, I know what I would think if a teenage girl came to me and told me the Holy Spirit made her pregnant.

Small towns can be both kind and cruel. So can children. I wonder if Jesus had to be the butt of ridicule and bear the label "bastard" when things got tough. Maybe His own earthly experiences helped Him to remember as He walked the streets and saw a lame man or a tax collector in a tree. The Gospels are full of Jesus' encounters with the invisible people of the time. Loneliness can be a fertility clinic for kindness, really.

I didn't know much about loneliness until I got to the city. Christmas followed my homeless night in Berlin. I had acquaintances, but no one with whom I could spend the holidays. I didn't have enough money to go home to the U.S. The time approaching Christmas Eve became excruciating. I was both desperate to find a place to spend Christmas and ashamed to let people know I had no place to go.

On Christmas Eve, I sat in my room at the student village as I listened to the laughter of people leaving with family or friends. I became aware that people as they passed could see that my light was still on. They would know that I had nowhere to go. I was afraid they would knock on my door and ask me what I was going to do. I quietly turned the light out and sat in the darkness on Christmas Eve, feeling more and more forlorn.

Finally, I got hold of myself as I sat in the dark. I said to myself, "Wait a minute. I'm not going to sit here passively. I can at least go to the place near the train station where I know all the beggars are and give them some money and good cheer on Christmas Eve, the poor things." I still didn't believe in God, but my heart was softening.

With a goal in mind, I felt strength return. I steeled myself to get on the subway alone and feign the appearance that I was going to some wonderful Christmas party. My spirits lifted as I got to the streets where the beggars always were. What a great feeling it would be to give out money and good cheer to the unfortunates. At least they were worse off than I was. How noble I really was!

Climbing out of the subway entrance, I felt my heart sink. The streets were absolutely empty. Not one person was on any of the corners where these poor people usually gathered. *Even the beggars have someplace to go on Christmas,* I thought. I roamed the deserted streets, pockets loaded with change that nobody needed, the loneliest young man in Berlin. I clenched my teeth, squeezed my eyes shut as hard as I could, and said to myself, "I never want to forget what this feels like." I ended up back in my room, alone.

At that time in my life, however, a tiny act of kindness took root like a tree. After the semester break, I was rushing around during a registration at the university in Berlin. The university was huge, the bureaucracy gigantic, the lines interminable, the language unfathomable. I felt I was treated not only as a number, a number printed on my foreign student I.D., but also as a stupid number, someone who could not understand instructions very well.

The students, like cattle, moved from station to station. I stood in line after line, as overworked administrators barked at me and the other students, because we were standing in the wrong lines. As I ran around trying to find teachers who might sign my registration card in a sea of students and harassed professors, one instructor did something remarkable.

He simply stopped in the middle of the chaos and looked me in the eye. He asked me my name. He asked me to have a seat. He listened to my responses. He asked, of all things, if I wanted a cigarette.

I didn't smoke, but somehow that offer of a cigarette melted a dam inside of me. It was a gesture of humanness, treating me like a peer rather than some foreign subspecies. I almost knelt at his feet and blubbered. I wasn't the most mature twenty-year-old on the block. That instructor will never know how that small gesture changed my life. Although I was an unbeliever at the time, somehow that act made me think that there was something beyond myself. It was a pointer on the road that eventually led me to Christ. I have almost totally forgotten the loneliness I felt, but that man's act of kindness continues to grow in me. After thirty years, I can see his face. I remember his name.

I returned to JFK airport in New York from Berlin over a year after I had left. Despite my great love for Berlin, the city had battered me and fed me a diet of anonymity. I was far more sensitive to the slightest hint of human kindness. Traveling from city to city with little money had worn me out. Cheap rooms and hostels had been my home for a while, often with people I did not know. I had not talked to an American for a long time.

Passing though customs in each country was always hard for me—waiting in lines and wondering if the officials would give me a problem. Then came the curt questions by overworked officers, possibly in another language. There was no time to be human or personal. Besides, to them I might be a smuggler. Any pause brought a wave of irritation from the anxious people waiting in line behind me.

The lines for customs at JFK airport were no different. The uniforms and the procedures were the same. People were rushing to get through. The customs officer went through my things efficiently. He looked at my passport, and at a glance he must have understood my story, my age, my time in Berlin and in other countries, how long I'd been away. He stopped his businesslike actions, looked me in the eye, and handed me my passport. With a beautiful Brooklyn accent, he said, "Welcome home." No sweeter words had ever reached my ears.

Kindness became more important to me. Without knowing it, that man paved the way for Christ. His small act of care made me tender to the possibility that invisible realities might lie beyond the visible facts around me. Perhaps life was more than what I thought I saw.

When I came to Christ not long afterward, I saw a little more. Often it is not the gifted speaker or slick media that bring people to Christ; it is the small thing. It is the man who stops for a moment from all the busyness and looks you in the eyes. I began to notice the woman on the corner who took her gloves off in the bitter cold so her new acquaintance could be warm. I caught for the first time the gesture of protectiveness, as a man in the park put a blanket over the shoulders of his girlfriend, shoulders that rested on a badly twisted back and useless, shriveled arms. Loneliness and heartache were the eyeglasses that helped me see those small deeds on the streets.

CHAPTER 4

Hiding and Revealing

Truly you are a God who hides himself.
ISAIAH 45:15 NIV

There is light enough for those who desire to see and darkness enough for those of a contrary disposition.
PASCAL

THROUGH A SERIES OF KIND ACTS, I came to know Christ after I left Berlin. Invisible threads drew me back to New York, then to Hong Kong, San Francisco, and finally again to New York. The experiences in Berlin had made me a little different from the self-absorbed kid with a backpack, wandering around Times Square.

Back in New York, working at a mission called Graffiti in the Lower East Side, I found myself constantly involved with people who knew the streets well and who often felt invisible. I saw small acts of kindness touch people who were desperately lonely in a way I could only vaguely remember. God and the city were not through with me yet.

Six days a week I thought it was important to look people in the eye. But on my day off when I walked the streets, I would wear sunglasses. I'd even wear them on the subway.

I didn't look cool in them. I was just a skinny white dude with some cheesy clip-ons. But I kept wearing the sunglasses because I loved to stare. I always have. I loved to walk and stare, especially at faces. I began telling my friends at our mission church, "There's no such thing as an ugly face." I'd usually get hoots, moans, and howls.

"Oh yes, there is such a thing!" they would shout. Then they would try to give some examples by pointing at someone or by naming names.

The examples never convinced me. With my sunglasses on, I could pick any face out on the street or in the subway. If I stared at a person's face long enough, something changed inside me. The face became noble, deep in sorrow and in challenges. Even expressions of anxiety or hurry or insecurity became part of the story. The ugliest face, if stared at for a few moments, became beautiful. Francis Schaeffer used to try to embody the biblical understanding of humanity by saying human beings are "magnificent even in ruin."[2] That phrase became a theme for me as I looked at people with my sunglasses on—a homeless man, a drug dealer, a harried shop owner. Perhaps ruined but still magnificent. The magnificence was just a little hidden.

Some faces captured my heart especially. Jake was a man who had a meal with us at our mission. His face was tanned and creased from living outside; his features were still chiseled and his hair was snow white. There was a tiny twinkle in his eyes. He was both shocked at life and wanted to tweak it at the same time. Jake's friend, John, accompanied him everywhere. "John's so famous, they named a room after him," Jake would say. John would usually remain silent and look off to the ceiling.

As time went on, I heard someone mention that John was actually Jake's son. "Jake, is John your son?" I asked, incredulously.

Jake hung his head as if the entire authority of the church universal had challenged his paternity. He looked up at me with a tormented look and said, "Well, I always *thought* he was, Pastor."

"Have a seat, Jake," I would tell him as he entered the storefront. "I have a seat," Jake would say. "Now I need a place to sit down."

As I got to know Jake, I wanted to tell him what a special person I thought he was. "If I were a painter, I'd paint your face, Jake."

He looked at me with hurt disbelief. "With what?" he asked, as if I had threatened him.

Remembering Berlin and living day to day in the city, I began to focus on faces rather than issues. When someone talked about homelessness, I saw Jake's face. When someone talked about mental illness, I saw John's. The people at our mission began to say to each other, "The bigger the city, the more personal we must become." This became a conviction. My experience in Berlin had made me suspect that we weren't seeing all there was to see.

As I thought about Jake and John, I began to search the Gospels again more eagerly. At the end of chapter 11 of Matthew, Jesus upbraided the cities because they refused to repent. Afterward, He gave the most wonderful invitation to those who are weary and worn out. In between these two segments, there is an amazing prayer: "I praise You, Father, Lord of heaven and earth, because You have hidden these things from the wise and learned and revealed them to infants" (Matt. 11:25). One of the things that Jesus thanks God for is that God both hides and reveals.

Working with inner-city kids, I began to think that God often showed things to the kids here at the mission and hid them from me. In Sunday school not long ago, one of the teachers shared about prayer. One of the boys was stunned. "You mean," he said, "that I don't even have to say the prayer out loud, that God knows what I am thinking? That He knows what is in my head even if I don't say it with my mouth?" The teacher nodded with bright encouragement. The little guy looked around with wide eyes. "Boy, am I in trouble!"

My heart became more sensitive to what might be happening around me. One Sunday, a boy came to church for the first time and sat on the front row. As the sermon began, the adults began to get that glazed look in their eyes.

"The Lord told Gideon he had too many men to fight, and twenty-two thousand men left!"

"D——!" the little boy exclaimed, on the edge of his seat, totally absorbed in this story he had never heard before. He was hanging on every word. He understood about fighting.

"And then out of the ten thousand that were left, the Lord only took three hundred!" I continued.

"D——!" the little boy said appreciatively again, his eyes getting bigger and bigger. His word was wrong, but his heart was on fire.

At every new twist in the story, the little boy shouted his enthusiastic response, totally unaware of the reaction around him. Finally, an adult crept over to instruct him to use some equally enthusiastic but more acceptable outburst. By that time the whole mission church was listening intently, hearing again for the first time, with a little child's ears, the amazing story.

Not long afterward, a little girl came up to me as she registered for our tutoring program. "I'm going to go to Holly Redeemer this Sunday to get confirmed," she bubbled.

Her mom, filling out forms, corrected her. "That's *Holy* Redeemer, Jessie."

"Whatever," Jessie said with a wave of her hand. Jessie looked at me with a roll of her eyes to include me in the knowledge that mothers just don't get it; then she ran off with a laugh to tell her friends about Holly.

How dull and sleepy-eyed adults get. Kids kept shaking me up and making me realize that the world was right before their eyes in ways hidden to me.

A short while after my talk with Jessie, I began to be anxious about a building project we were working on. I simply could not see where the money would come from for the next step, and the deadlines were bearing down on the construction team. I, the pastor, sat down with our construction manager to see what we could do. It was right before the Christmas holidays and I was exhausted. I suppose my face showed all my fears.

"Don't worry, Taylor" the construction manager said, who was not prone to being pastoral or to talking about God. "Our Father has all the resources of the world." He spread his big hands as wide as he could. "He will provide what we need exactly when we need it." He, the construction manager, was telling me, the pastor, to trust God more and not depend merely on the facts I saw. I was blessed because of what God had revealed to him and concealed from me, probably because I thought I knew all the answers.

Children, construction workers, and people who ate with us all became the ones who showed me what I wasn't seeing. "You never know who God might use to speak through!" Jake shouted at me the next Wednesday at our meal. "Remember Balaam and his ass. If God could speak through Balaam's ass, He might even speak through me!"

No matter how routine or boring a day might be, no matter how dreadful the talks might seem, I saw that God is both concealer and revealer. What He may not have allowed me to see yesterday He may reveal to me today and probably through someone or something I would never have imagined.

When I stopped thinking I knew it all because I had a seminary degree, God began to use more and more unexpected people to show how much was hidden from my sight. For example, a group of people gathered to do visitation to help start another outreach group in the Lower East Side. We were pairing off two by two. I could see what was shaping up. I was going to be paired with Marty, who could not see. He wore dark glasses and carried a red cane. I had nothing against Marty, but I knew the building we were going to visit. At that time, several people had pit bull dogs there, and a vicious German shepherd frequently got loose on the third floor. I just wanted to be able to run if I needed to run, and I didn't think Marty could keep up.

Marty graciously pretended not to notice my reluctance. We knocked on the door of the man with the pit bull. The man opened the door a crack and glared at us. I looked at the pit bull and kept my ears cocked for the rustling of the German shepherd upstairs.

"Hi. We're starting a group down the street, and I just wanted you to know you're invited and we'd love for you to come. We'll see you later." I was ready to move on. The pit bull began to growl as the man pushed him back with his foot.

But Marty was just getting started. "Did you grow up on this block?" he asked. He started talking to the man forcefully. Soon areas of sin and addiction were laid bare in the man's life as Marty shared what Christ had done in his own life. "When I was using drugs, I never saw how *stupid* I was," he said with a booming voice that shook the hallway. Both Marty and the man began to speak loudly.

"Marty, let's go," I said, trying to pull him away. The pit bull had wedged half of his huge head through the doorway and was raising the level of his growl. He moved the door farther open in short spurts, twisting like an alligator.

Marty kept at it. He was touching sensitive places of truth in the man's life. Finally, the man waved his hand. "Ah, you're nothing but a blind guy."

With his blank, sincere eyes, Marty looked squarely into the face of the other man, who could only scowl and squint. Marty was forceful and clear. "I may be blind, but I see more than you do." Both the man and I stepped back. Even the pit bull stopped pushing. Marty was speaking the truth. He was seeing things that the man and I were not seeing.

G. K. Chesterton once described contentment in this way: "the power of getting out of any situation all that there is in it."[3] After being with Marty, I wondered, was I seeing all I could from the situations around me? As I walked the streets of my city, I began to think how God might reveal things to me from the corner I had passed a thousand times. What my own obtuseness and self-centeredness may have helped hide God may reveal to me in an instant.

Wonder of all wonders, for the one who reads the Bible, is that God hides Himself. "Truly you are a God who hides himself" (Isa. 45:15 NIV). For a Christian these words make a strange kind of sense. It is hard to see God's working through a feeding trough in a barn. It is hard to imagine the Son of God coming as the son of a carpenter in an oppressed colony, without a home or a steady job. In the Garden of Gethsemane, even Jesus struggled in seeing God's action on the cross, yet what an astonishing work. As I saw the heartache and the abuse on the streets, I was struck by the kernel of truth that came from the rough shells of these experiences. Who knows where God is hiding?

Jake recounted an old rabbi's story on one Wednesday night. He said, "Do you know the feeling when you are a child and play hide-and-seek? Have you ever gone off to hide and the other children got tired of the game and went away but forgot to tell you? It is a terrible feeling. That is what God feels." I had never seen Jake so serious.

Examples of God's hiding and revealing began to leap out at me from all over the Bible. At another point in Isaiah, God says, "I was ready to answer my people's prayers, but they did not pray. I was ready for them to find me, but they did not even try. The nation did not pray to me, even though I was always ready to answer, 'Here I am, I will help you'" (Isa. 65:1 TEV). I kept thinking of the picture of God waiting for His people to find Him. I thought about Jake's life. I even wondered if he had hid as a child, waiting for someone to find him.

A Christian never brings God to any area, and especially not to the inner city. God is always already there, even if He is concealed. I thought I was doing OK "bringing" God to my first group of teenage boys at the storefront, until Joey started kicking in the door. As the metal on the door cracked and buckled, I felt too inadequate to do anything. I didn't really have a lot in common with Joey. I was quiet and into reading poetry. Joey was furious and into destroying property. As Joey screamed in rage, I silently thought that perhaps it was time to find a better match for my talents. All I could see was a tough, angry teenager.

Yet I continued, and Joey's erratic behavior continued. It wasn't easy. During one rare quiet moment, I took him to a store. On a whim, I bought him a little plastic puzzle with a Bible verse on it.

Joey didn't seem to be changing for the better. He acted tougher as he got older. He wasn't the type to show much affection. But people continued to love him at Graffiti, the mission church. Three long years later, he was the first person in his family of drug dealers to graduate from high school. No one was prouder of him than I was. I was beginning to see a little more of who Joey was. Before he graduated, I met him on the street. He acted tough, but he looked around to see if anyone was watching. He pulled out something he kept hidden in his pocket. He said, "I still remember."

It was the faded, worn plastic puzzle I had given him three years before. It looked as though he carried it in his pocket every day. On it I could still read the faded letters, "For God so loved the world . . ."

At that time I couldn't speak, I was so bowled over. But I can speak now. I saw something through what Joey had hidden in his pocket. I learned through Joey that I don't have to be an expert on juvenile development to make a difference in someone's life. I saw that there were hundreds of kids just blocks from where I work who were secretly looking for that golden person who knows each one's name.

And I saw something about God. God had been doing work under my nose that was so very hidden from me. As God was mending Joey of his anger and abuse, He was mending me of my shyness and my mere head knowledge. The blood began to flow around my heart, not just around my head.

It was happening there all the time on my street corner. I just needed to see it.

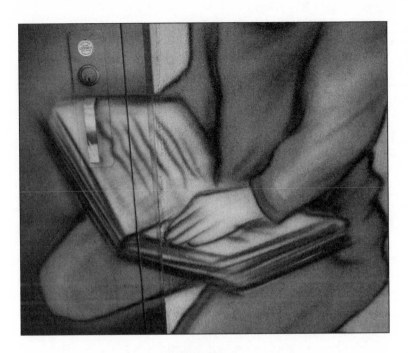

CHAPTER 5

The Two Books of God

Wisdom calls aloud in the street,
she raises her voice in the public squares;
at the head of the noisy streets she cries out,
in the gateways of the city she makes her speech.

PROVERBS 1:20–21 NIV

People see God every day, they just don't recognize him.

PEARL BAILEY

25

SOMETHING WAS IN THE AIR. Things were changing. I was sitting on the front stoop next to the storefront mission where I worked. I looked down the street and felt the morning breeze. Even the air smelled fresher. The neighborhood was a little different. No longer were all the young people immediately beginning to deal drugs as soon as they had a chance. The system of darkness that held these streets in its grip was just beginning to lift. One big teenager rushed up to me. His father was a drug dealer. With wide eyes, he announced, "I need a Bible."

I was thrilled beyond speaking. Never before had any teenager ever come up to me on the street and said, "I need a Bible."

"Well, what kind do you want?" I asked. I was thinking of possibilities—a New Testament, a full Bible, big print, pictures, pocket-size, NIV, TEV, and on and on.

He looked at me as if I were a complete idiot. "The *Holy* Bible," he said with righteous disdain. Stupid me.

It is holy. No need to get into a doctrinal debate here. As a reader, I know that the Bible is like no other book I have ever read. Wondrous, compelling, probing. Sometimes as I read the Bible, it takes me by the hand. Sometimes when I read, it grabs me by the neck. It is holy.

George Mueller, the Christian who trusted God to provide for thousands of orphans each day, gave some advice for those whose Bible study times seemed dry. He said that he would read his Bible while he was on his knees. His body position reminded him of the awesome wonder of meeting God through reading His Word.

As God and the city began to change my sight, I began to read the Bible differently. Sometimes in my office, a remodeled bedroom in a building that was once abandoned, I knelt as I did my Bible study. As I faced the brick wall and the pigeons gathered around the window, cooing and clucking, I remembered what is important.

In the front of my Bible, I keep a quote from Erasmus when he first printed a Greek New Testament: "These holy pages will summon up the living image of His mind. They will give you Christ Himself, talking, healing, dying, rising, the whole Christ in a word;

they will give Him to you in an intimacy so close that He would be less visible to you if He stood before your eyes."[4] By reading God's Word, we see the living Savior, who, among many other things, is a walker of the streets of the city. Sometimes those reformers, who read the Bible so carefully, called the Bible "spectacles" with which we could see the world around us.

The Bible is like a set of eyeglasses, a set of shades. It helps us to see. Ad Reinhardt, an artist in New York in the 1960s, painted black paintings repetitiously through his life. He commented on what he did: "Looking is not as simple as it looks."[5] Whatever my take on a black painting might be, I do have one thing in common with this artist. Sometimes we have to learn to see. The Bible helps me do that.

Some of the early Christians used the phrase "the two books of God." The one book of God for Christians is, of course, the Bible. The other book is nature, all that is made, which continues to teach and instruct us in God's ways. Paul, to show that we are without excuse in knowing God, says "since the creation of the world God's invisible qualities—his eternal power and divine nature—have been clearly seen, being understood from what has been made" (Rom. 1:20 NIV).

I began to understand more clearly that the city is a part of nature too. In a sense, I read the book of God every time I step out onto the street. In the Scripture at the beginning of this chapter, Proverbs reminds us that wisdom is in the streets, of all places.

I don't think that nature is just brooks and streams. "Nature, who made the mason, made the house,"[6] Emerson once said. When I look at the house, I see the housebuilder and the One who created the housebuilder. For me, God made the people who made the city, as God made the bird that made the nest. Nature is all we see as we walk the streets of the city. It's a gigantic nest.

My friend who hikes on mountain trails is not impressed. "So what if it's a part of nature? So what if the city's like a nest? Look how the city has fouled its own nest! The smog, the garbage, the smells."

"I'm as much a nature lover as you are," I would counter in our ongoing discussions. "I'm just trying to see the big picture. You call yourself a nature lover, but your nature is getting smaller and smaller. I just want to learn to see the good here," I say, sounding unconvinced.

"The only good that comes out of New York City is I–95," mumbles my friend. "It's a place of crime and greed and pollution."

"Like I haven't heard *this* before," I complain, raising my hand to the ceiling. "Why don't you try to hike the city like you do the mountains? You won't meet a bear, but you might get chased by a mugger in a fur coat. If you think of each building as a giant red-wood tree, you're walking through a huge, majestic forest. Or think of the choices you make on the street as the kind of choice you make when you decide to take a piece of fruit off a tree on the trail."

"Yeah, yeah, I tried that," my friend would say. "I took a bite out of the Big Apple, but it had a worm in it. I spent the day choking fumes in a subway station. You'll have to take that kind of hike on your own."

I will.

The Bible reminds us that not only mountains and trees are wondrous but also streets and towers. The lyrics of one of the songs the people of God used to sing tell us to walk around the city:

Number her towers,

consider well her ramparts, go through her citadels;

that you may tell the next generation that this is God,

our God for ever and ever. (Ps. 48:12b–14a RSV)

The towers and structures are not a sign of the evils of the city; they are a cause for wonder.

One of the themes of our mission comes from Isaiah 61:4. The people God renews, it says, will rebuild the city. After my friend left for the country, I read the Isaiah passage again. I looked around at the abandoned buildings in my part of the city and I asked, "What does it mean to rebuild the city?" Surely, just as Isaiah,

Nehemiah, Ezra, Haggai, and Zechariah showed us, physical construction sometimes had to be done in the city. The streets, the walls, the temples, the dwelling places were all a part of the physical rebuilding of the city. But I knew in my heart that the rebuilding meant something more.

Once I realized that, a man, whom I'll call Jamie, became my teacher concerning rebuilding. He was an unabashed alcoholic and lived in the park.

"Give me some money," he would plead. He knew my name, but he looked right through me. I was a possible means to an end; I was an object that might help him get another bottle. He wandered the park in his skinny, frail body, a ghost, a prisoner confined not by walls.

Once, during a thunderstorm, I remember leaving the storefront. There was Jamie, standing like a specter, totally wet, oblivious to everything around him. He saw me.

"Please come in out of the rain," I begged. "This is crazy, Jamie."

Jamie looked right through me. He held out his hand. "All I need is a dollar," he said. "Just give me a dollar."

"I can't do that," I said. "But come inside. Maybe I can find some dry clothes."

"How about fifty cents?" Jamie asked. "That would help me on the way."

"I can't do that," I stuttered. "But just step inside out of the rain, Jamie."

"Just a quarter. Please. That's all I ask." His look was so desperate. He was so wet and cold. But he refused all my offers. We both knew what he wanted.

I went inside for a moment, and when I came out, I saw Jamie sitting on a cement block on the sidewalk in the pouring rain. He was vomiting out everything left in his stomach, and the heavy rain washed it all across the sidewalk. As I stood next to him in the pouring rain, a wave of exhaustion and despair washed over me. "Nothing will ever change," a voice said inside me. "This is the reality of the streets. Everything you do is useless." I finally left him there, squatting in the downpour, a wet stray cat, stubborn, huffing and spraying the last of his insides onto the streets.

But time is also a servant of the Lord. I have known alcoholics who have said the words to ask Christ into their hearts a hundred times. But as they look back on their lives, the moment of conversion for them was when faith worked deep inside them and they took the step to change the situation. Jamie took the step to go to a rehabilitation program and stopped drinking. He went to a place in the country that our mission sponsored. Surrendering to Christ was not easy for him. He cried to the Lord from the depths of his heart. Slowly, day by day, his heart and his body mended.

When he returned and came to our storefront to eat a meal, time stopped. Forks froze halfway to mouths. Coffee cups were never placed back on the table. Every rowdy street person stopped talking to look at one of the most famous drunks in the neighborhood. His eyes were clear; his hands were steady. No sermon I had ever preached, no theological nicety I had ever phrased had a fraction of the impact of Jamie, simply walking through the door. Eyes that had long been closed to God blinked open with an animal instinct that something new and unusual had happened. Later Jamie helped us prepare a site for the construction of a new building. He stood tall and looked me in the eye with a smile.

I thought about the first book of God, the Holy Bible, which told us the people of the Spirit would rebuild the city. As Jamie held a shovel and laughed with me, I looked at his face and saw another story of God's work in the city, a second book of God.

He was a walking Bible for everyone to see, and his work with a shovel shouted hope on the streets. Without knowing it, he taught me to read the book of God better than any professor ever had.

CHAPTER 6

The Best and the Worst of You

Search me, O God, and know my heart;
test me and know my anxious thoughts.

PSALM 139:23 NIV

The city will bring out the best and the worst in you.

COMMON SAYING ON THE STREET

HERE IS A STORY I'M NOT SO PROUD OF. Steven was violent and usually drunk. He was smart enough to know he could cause a lot of trouble when he wanted to. He drifted in and out of our lives at the mission in New York City. I imagine he drifted in and out of the lives of his drinking buddies too. I personally couldn't conceive of anyone putting up with him for long in his usual state of mind.

Every Wednesday night before Thanksgiving, we have a special Thanksgiving meal at a larger location, so we can include a larger group of people. Like clockwork, each year, some especially drunk person shows up and attempts to disrupt the evening. We can count on it.

On one of those evenings, Steven showed up. My heart sank. Things seemed to be getting harder in the neighborhood for me, rather than easier. "Get out of my way!" Steven shouted and spit. "This is the worst church in the neighborhood!" he bellowed to people walking by. He began to flail his arms and careened dangerously toward one of the workers. "Let me in!" he shouted as he pushed the person at the door. "I'm going to beat every one of you up." He stuck his fist, big as a mutton roast, in my face. His breath was ignitable. "I'm not leaving until you call the police!" he announced at the top of his voice, with a determined, alcoholic exuberance. Our special guest for the night. "All guests . . . should be welcomed as Christ,"[7] the Benedictines tell us. Well, welcome, Jesus.

There were a hundred things to do inside, but since I knew Steven the best, I was the best bet to get him away without total disruption of the meal. "Come on, Steven," I said, "let's walk over here and talk together." Suspiciously, he lunged along with me down the block, seeming to float on the power of his own breath.

As we walked away from the building and talked, Steven became vaguely aware that he was ceasing to be the center of attention, and he deeply resented me and the universe for that fact. By the time we had gotten to the park two blocks away, the full realization of his neutralization as the destroyer of our night hit him.

He stopped at the edge of the park, weaving and cursing at me furiously. "I'm not staying here," he hissed. "I'm going right back to the church. They're going to have to let me in, or I'm going to punch every one of them out." Every word gushed out with a powerful slurred vehemence. "You watch me. You're going to have to call the police. I won't let anyone eat!" His face screwed up in an ugly mask of inebriated fury. He tried to stab at my face with his elbow but missed. He reversed his direction and lurched back toward the church. I was amazed at his bulldog determination.

At that moment, his right foot did not go where he had planned it to go. Like a ship in a huge wave, he rolled sideways toward the ground. There was a muffled crack as his head hit the sidewalk. He was out cold.

I stood there in the quiet, dark park, staring at him. There were already more than a hundred people waiting for me at the church. I was supposed to start an evangelical program and lead a prayer in a few minutes.

I stood still in the dark, undecided about what to do. A few years earlier, I would have cradled this man's head, called the ambulance, and spent the next two hours trying to help him.

But my eyes were adjusting to dark places. I was fairly certain that if I called an ambulance, it would come and paramedics would spend a great deal of time and energy (and money) to revive him. Steven would, however, refuse to go to the hospital, regardless of his condition. The ambulance call would be a waste, plus I would have a newly revived Steven, with all his determination to go and punch people at our church.

Steven was breathing regularly on the sidewalk. I really did not want him to awaken. I did not want him to see me when he woke up either. My presence would only inflame his ire and remind him of his mission.

So I made the choice and left him. I just walked away. I secretly hoped no one saw me abandon the poor man in his apparent need on the sidewalk. But I felt I would be a better shepherd to him and my people if I left him rather than staying to cradle his head in my arms.

I'm still not sure I did the right thing. What would Jesus do? Either choice would be inconsiderate to someone.

The choices we make in the dark are different once our eyes have adjusted. People bring choices. Lots of people in one place put you in contact with many choices, and you are forced to make many decisions. These decisions help you see yourself. I think I'm a wonderful person when I am all alone in a cabin in the country. It is only when I must face people, and sometimes hostile people, that I am forced to look at myself.

I saw Steven several days later. He bore no marks from the night and, of course, remembered nothing about his hostility or my abandonment of him.

That was fine with me.

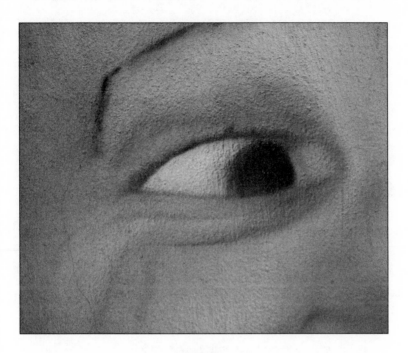

CHAPTER 7

All Eye

[H]aving the eyes of your hearts enlightened.
EPHESIANS 1:18 RSV

We can see only what we have grown an eye to see.
E. F. SCHUMACHER

INWARDLY, I HAD CHANGED SOME from my first night of deep sleep in a flophouse at Times Square. I had seen so much hope in the people God had called, but I'd also had my share of discouragements. After years in the city, I found myself sick of Manhattan. It was almost Christmas Eve, and icy rains had been coming down all morning. All the other workers at the mission had gone home for Christmas. We had three hundred sandwiches to give out, and people were crowding around the door of our storefront. The line writhed like a wet snake—everyone wanted to cut in line to escape the snowy slush all around.

I stood at the front of the door, soaked to the bone, irritable, tired, and angry. At that moment, I hated the city. I worked to keep people in line until the inexperienced helpers inside were ready. The homeless man at the front of the line had a dark blue stocking cap on, pulled down over his forehead. "Please stand over here, sir," I said. He obediently stepped to the side. I continued to stand there and defend the doorway. The man in the cap at the front of the line looked at me. I looked at him. It wasn't that I didn't like him; it was just that he was not important at that time. He wasn't causing a problem, so he wasn't warranting my attention.

He looked at me again, and I smiled a forced smile at him as I noticed an older man and his friend cutting in front of a group of older ladies. "Stop that!" I shouted irritably.

Finally, the man next to me took a step forward, looked me in the eye, smiled, and shook my hand vigorously. I gave him a limp handshake while I wondered when the blasted sandwiches would be ready. "Please stand next to the wall so we don't block the side-walk!" I bleated to someone farther down the line. Then, after about twenty minutes of standing next to this quiet gentleman with the blue stocking cap, my eyes rested for a moment on his chin. I continued to look at his chin as he continued to look down. Slowly, in the rain, I lowered my head so that I could look at his mouth. I lowered my head to look at his nose. I kept lowering my head, as walls collapsed inside my mind until I saw his twinkling eyes.

It was my best friend from college and from seminary. We had roomed together in college and in seminary and had lived together helping to start a ministry in Harlem. We had spent hundreds and hundreds of hours together, days at a time, nonstop. He had come in from another part of the country and had sneaked into our clothing closet, got some old clothes, and waited in line for his sandwich. I had stood next to my best friend for twenty minutes, looked him in the face numerous times, shook his hand, spoke to him, but did not see him. He had been invisible to me, even though I thought I'd learned so much about how that felt.

I hugged my friend and sputtered. I was delighted and embarrassed to see him. I was embarrassed because I had been so stupid and because I had been so cranky with all those people in front of my friend.

I was also humbled. Before I became a Christian, I took fiendish pleasure in the stories in Luke and John in which people did not recognize Jesus. "See," I would proclaim, "it must have been someone else. They didn't recognize him." But now I know that if something isn't in our anticipated category, no matter how obvious it is, we probably won't see it.

There is an ancient Christian saying that says the Christian brother or sister must be "all eye." On many days, I have been mostly mouth. I think of the tens of thousands of people, the thousands of faces, I have looked at but not seen. I think of the thousands of hands that have reached out to take mine, and I have seen right through them. Perhaps the Easter stories in which people don't recognize Jesus are in the Gospels to remind us that the resurrected Lord still walks among us, and we still do not see Him.

That is why, every day, I receive Paul's prayers for the believers, that the eyes of our hearts be enlightened (Eph. 1:18). There is so much more to see than I ever knew.

Reflection: Jesus

The Spitter
Mark 8:22–26

Jesus spit on him. That was the first thing He did. He must have found the blind man on the street, led him outside the town, and spit on his eyes. You might say that's a poor way to help someone see.

But not really.

The man had begged Jesus to touch him. Jesus had taken him by the hand, and after He spit on him, He laid his hands on him. That should be the end of the story. The man should be healed, like all the other blind people who recovered their sight in the Bible.

But not really.

The man only saw a little bit. People were more like walking trees than like people. There were stages. It took time. Jesus didn't seem frustrated. He lay His hands on the man's eyes. It says the man looked intently. We don't know for how long. Maybe for a long time. Finally, the man saw everything clearly.

You might think that's the end of the story, but you've got to read the next story about Peter and the whole chapter and the whole book. Even with Jesus being right there, recovery of sight didn't always come all at once. Even with miracles, there may be stages. You might think helping that poor man physically see was for sure the most important thing Jesus did at that time.

But not really.

Street Furniture

(SEEING THE RICHES THAT ARE ALREADY OURS

AS INHERITORS OF CITY SURROUNDINGS)

CHAPTER 8

The Tree That Started a Conversion

In the midst of the street of it, and on either side of the river, was there the tree of life.

REVELATION 22:2A KJV

Without trees, cities are just a scab on the landscape.

PRINTED ON A CARD IN A NEIGHBORHOOD STORE

"IT'S RIGHT THERE. Can't you see it? It's right under your nose."

I would look at whatever the collection was in front of me—tools, food, papers, signs—but I could not see the thing I needed. "No," I would shout.

"If it were a snake, it would bite you!"

My eyes would scan the array of items, but I would see nothing. "I still can't see it," I would say.

Finally, the person would walk over and pick it up. Sure enough, it was right in front of me. I just couldn't see it.

As I continued to live in the city for a longer time, I began to realize there were things that were always there, things that I used, that I depended on, but which I never saw—trees, animals, storefronts, sidewalks, walls, systems. They were simply "street furniture," objects that were there but were taken for granted.

Once I began to see these objects, it was as though someone walked over and pointed them out in the middle of an entire display. They were right in front of me all the time.

David describes Jerusalem as "a city that is closely compacted together" (Ps. 122:3 NIV). It is a city where everything "is bound firmly together" (NRSV), "a city restored in beautiful order and harmony" (TEV). I knew what it was like to live in the city, but I never noticed the parts "closely compacted together" that make up a city.

As I walked down Avenue B in our neighborhood, the August air smothered me like a fur coat in a sauna. I looked up the avenue. It looked like nothing more than a giant concrete ravine. Air conditioners dotted the walls, belching out even more heat into a street that already felt like an oven. A haze of smog enveloped the stoplight on the corner.

Every garbage can struck out at the passing pedestrians with a toxic, rancid smell. The smell of human urine and dog feces billowed along the sidewalk.

People sat on the stoops, trying to find a spot where a little shade from the building ledges might give them a moment's respite. They were neither talking nor moving; their bodies had shifted into a motionless survival mode. Any emotion at all usually erupted like a pustule of irritation. I stared down this brick canyon, choked with smog, and I saw the streets of the city as hot, hostile, hellish.

Standing there, sweating, I saw clearly what was missing.

Trees. The park in the neighborhood had been closed because of a violent difference of opinion between the government and some residents. People had always gone to the park to cool down, and now they were restrained by an eight-foot fence. Trees were the lungs and air conditioners of the neighborhood, and now we couldn't get close to them.

Suddenly, now that they were barricaded, trees became very important to me. The cool cluster of trees beyond the chain-link fence were tantalizing. The trees on the inside of the fence waved their green arms at the sluggish people as they passed by. The park with the trees was ten degrees cooler than the street where the residents stood. Trees had silently given oxygen and coolness to all of us, and we had never noticed.

Noticing trees in the city around me as I walked the streets, I began to notice them in the Bible too. They were everywhere. The tree of the knowledge of good and evil and the tree of life were at the beginning of the human drama in the Bible (Gen. 2:17; 3:22). At the end of the Bible, at the end of time and space as we know it, there is no more temple, but in the middle of the new city, sure enough, there is a tree, and its leaves are for the healing of the peoples (Rev. 22:2).

For Christians, in the center of human history, there is a tree. What was a curse became a blessing for everyone: "He himself bore our sins in his body on the tree, so that we might die to sins and live for righteousness" (1 Pet. 2:24 NIV; see also Gal. 3:13; Acts 10:39). A friend gave me a book with a computer printout of all the Scriptures that have the word *tree* in it. The book was huge.

Once you think about something, you begin to see it everywhere. Brother Lawrence's small book *The Practice of the Presence of God* has blessed many Christians for generations. This simple

45

man, who washed pots and pans in his community, rested in the presence of God so deeply that people were drawn to him.

It was stunning to read again the story of his conversion. This is the description of Lawrence's coming to God:

> I met Brother Lawrence for the first time today.
> He told me that God had been especially good to
> him in his conversion. He was eighteen at the time,
> and still in the world. He told me that it had all hap-
> pened one winter day, as he was looking at a barren
> tree. Although the tree's leaves were indeed gone, he
> knew that they would soon reappear, followed by
> blossoms and then fruit. This gave him a profound
> impression of God's providence and power which
> never left him. Brother Lawrence still maintains that
> this impression detached him entirely from the
> world and gave him such a great love for God that it
> hasn't changed in all of the forty years he has been
> walking with Him.[8]

Can really seeing a tree change you? For Lawrence at eighteen, it was not reading a book, watching a video, reading a tract, seeing a TV show, or listening to a Christian CD. It was looking at a barren tree.

Trees are giving and forgiving, silently blessing us and asking very little in return. In the final analysis, trees could live without humans, but humans could not live without trees.

We have a backyard that is eight feet wide and twenty feet long. When we moved to our tenement apartment on the ground floor, our backyard was a stretch of hard-packed dirt, punctuated by old bricks and broken glass.

Slowly, we worked to make it more livable. We spent hours picking up the endless collection of broken glass. We found a "Tree of Heaven" growing out of the side of a wall. Many people call this a "weed tree," but we admired its bulldog-like desire to live. We carefully dislodged it and planted it in our backyard. In a world of brick and concrete, one little sliver of tree became very precious. It was only about two feet tall, but I would look out the window in order to watch it in all kinds of seasons. Our boys ripped off several of its few branches; for me, it was like seeing the fingers of a child broken off. The tree still grew.

We loved that pathetic little tree and nurtured it, until it was much taller than I was. Its trunk was thickening and its branches leaped a few feet higher each year. It seemed well on its way to having a place. When our landlord, without notice, had our backyard covered with cement, Susan, my wife, persuaded the construction workers to leave a little square open, hardly a foot wide, so our precious little tree could keep growing.

One winter day some utility men were in the backyard. The long stick of the tree didn't look like much to them in this little back alley. My wife watched one of them casually reach up and break the tree in two. Joking with his friend, he found a plastic owl on the ground (there in a vain attempt to scare away pigeons and rodents) and set the plastic owl on top of the broken stump.

My wife was angry. Why would someone destroy something we had nurtured for so long for no apparent reason? Why crucify and humiliate this poor little tree? It was now only a broken stump with no branches, about four feet tall. After many phone calls to many supervisors, the utility company agreed to give us $600 to have any tree we wanted planted in its place. This process of conversation took months. "What kind of tree should we put in, Susan? A pin oak, a cherry tree, or a pear tree?" Our grief was diverted by the excitement of something new and expensive.

On Easter morning that year, I looked out our back window. There was the forlorn stump of our tree, still sticking out of the ground, surrounded by old buildings and cement.

But it wasn't dead. Stupid me. There was a little green sprout coming out of the place that was broken. I remembered a quote from Ernest Hemingway: "The world breaks every one and afterward many are strong at the broken places."[9] This little tree was becoming strong in the place that seemed like an amputation.

Susan and I stared at the tree and then looked at each other. "Let's forget the fancy tree," I told Susan. "This tree is far more important. It is a resurrection tree." Now our tree is three times as tall as I am, with a gnarled place where it was broken off, but strong and tall.

We seldom value something unless it is seen to be rare. Crowded cities can make trees seem rare and precious. Even though it may take us an hour to get to Central Park, it is worth it to be among a gathering of trees. Once on a picnic there, my young boys wanted to climb a tree, so I helped them up into a tree with low branches. Then I climbed up myself. This was a rare treat for children who knew mostly sidewalks and buildings.

A small but vigorous old lady promptly emerged from a group of trees and informed us that climbing trees in Central Park was illegal. Because there are so many people, permission to climb the trees might eventually destroy them. She had no uniform on, but she spoke with authority. She obviously loved trees. Chastised and disappointed, the three of us slithered down.

Central Park is huge. Several months later, thirty blocks north of our last picnic in the park, the temptation to give the boys and myself a chance to get in a tree was too much for me. Honestly, I had forgotten about the old lady. My memory was quickly refreshed. As soon as I had gotten one of my sons up in the tree, the same lady emerged out of nowhere and gave me exactly the same speech. Defying all odds, her shocking appearance, like Elijah's, humbled us into submission. We have never climbed a tree again in Central Park. Even a tree needs a guardian sometimes.

Each week some of the workers at our mission gather together to pray and plan. Each week someone reads a story or a Scripture. I've forgotten most of them. One, however, stands out in my mind. It is the story of a tree.

My coworker, who has had a rough life herself, read a story from a book she brought. In the story, a person looks at a tree and sees a place where it had been broken and damaged. Yet that damage had not completely stopped its growth. The outer covering of the tree had partially grown around the wound. Old dead wood from the damage was still visible, but it had been worn by time. The channel for nutrients for the tree had found a way to grow over and around the trauma.

In the story, the tree had grown far above and beyond the wound. Green leaves brought shade and coolness to the area around the tree. After reading this, my coworker shared some of the sadness in her own life and the hope she had. She hoped that even with her broken parts, she could be like that tree and still grow to bless others.

The people in our group became silent. We knew what she hoped had come true. She had become like that tree.

There is a tree outside our apartment building that is barely making it. It is rarely noticed. It has had branches ripped off by kids and teenagers passing by who aren't even thinking. Pet owners have let their dogs urinate on the tiny patch of ground where the tree grows up through the sidewalk, not knowing that this treatment is deadly to a tree. It has been treated casually, like street furniture, instead of being treated like a living thing. Bikers chain their bikes to its young trunk, not knowing that their chains are destroying the outer layers of the tree, the place where the water and the nutrients move. Yet leaves still appear on its branches. It continues to overcome and provide feeble shade for kids, teenagers, dog owners, and bikers.

By watching the trees on my street, I've become a little more streetwise. The trees, like us, are affected by thoughtlessly inflicted damage. Yet, through God's care, life continues to thrive. A tree's life helps our lives, even when we don't realize it. If we looked at trees more, perhaps they could help us in our own conversion. I've learned that trees don't say much, and they don't really have to.

CHAPTER 9

Animal Kingdom

*"And should I not be concerned about Nineveh, that
great city, in which there are more than a hundred and
twenty thousand persons who do not know their right
hand from their left, and also many animals?"*

JONAH 4:11 NRSV

*[Other animals] are not brethren, they are not under-
lings; they are other nations, caught with ourselves in the
net of life and time, fellow prisoners of the splendor and
travail of the earth.*

ON A BRONZE STATUE IN ZAMBIA

THE COUPLE SQUATTED NEXT TO the building and begged. The woman had a nail through her lip. She had a canvas hat with no brim over her matted hair. Her pants looked purposefully ripped. Her skin looked chalky, as if she had slept in an inch of fine dust. Her boots went up to her knees, with little metal studs around the edge. She was probably seventeen.

The young man looked as though he was about the same age. He had a black scarf around his neck and a row of metal spikes in his ear. He wore a dirty T-shirt with no sleeves and ripped-up jeans. He wore a vacant stare as he asked people passing by for change.

In between them sat a dog. Next to the dog was a bowl of water. The dog was a young pit bull with mottled brown markings. It had a collar with spikes on it. It sat with its tongue out, breathing heavily.

The dog was the key.

"Hi, my name's Taylor," I said as I squatted down to talk to the man and the woman.

Vacant stares.

"I live in the neighborhood. What's your name?" I pressed on.

No eye contact. Finally the young man spoke. "Ax," he said. This outpouring of expression seemed to have exhausted him. I wasn't sure whether his response was a verb or a noun. He looked through me to another man passing by. "Got any spare change?" he shouted at the man's back.

Long pause. "May I pet your dog?" I asked.

A grunt, which I took for a yes.

I began petting the dog, which licked my hand. "Nice markings," I said. The dog began to push my hand with his nose. "Hey, this dog's got personality." The first faint flicker of interest from Ax. The young woman looked at the dog with motherly pride. "What's his name?" I ventured.

"Killer." She spoke for the first time.

I continued to pet the dog, hyphenating the name of the man and the dog together in my mind. "I bet Killer is a good watchdog," I said.

"The best," she responded with more enthusiasm. "Even if someone walks by the door of our squat, he lets us know. No one ever tries to mess with our stuff, 'cause of Killer. Isn't that right, Killer?" She spoke as she rubbed the place underneath his spiked collar. "We picked him up from a friend for only ten dollars. We'd never let go of him." On and on she talked about Killer with maternal enthusiasm and unabashed love.

The dog was the key.

My friend, Kareem, realized it too. He got a donation of dog biscuits and began to walk around with them. Giving a biscuit to a dog seemed to open the mouths of the owners.

We were standing on a street corner as we gave out sandwiches one day. There was a doctor giving medical pre-screenings.

"Don't mess with someone's dog," I said to a group helping that day as we stood on the street. "You can hit the person, curse at them, betray them, but if you abuse the dog, then you've broken the ultimate taboo. A lot of the squatters have dogs."

"Why not have a medical prescreening for dogs?" someone said. "We could get some veterinarians from some churches."

"We could have a sign that said the Church Is Going to the Dogs on the front," one bystander said. The wise-guy poetry of that headline compelled us to bring it about.

We called it "Dog Day Afternoon," and it was an insurance nightmare. Eighty dogs and cats were gathered together on the street for our first animal event. I figured that any minute a pit bull was going to swallow a Chihuahua like an hors d'oeuvre.

The pets and their owners from the neighborhood were, of course, ecstatic. It was like dog and cat disco, with a swarm of four-legged friends sniffing each other and barking and meowing. The dogs were wriggling out of their skins in social anticipation.

As I watched this swarming sea of tails, I came to realize that the city is also made up of animals. We willingly feed, coddle, and nurture some animals. Other animals we can't get rid of. These animals live off us in the city in spite of ourselves.

At the end of the Book of Jonah, God wants Jonah to know that he is not only concerned about the people in the city of Nineveh but also about the many animals (cattle). By doing a medical prescreening for animals, I began to see not only dogs and cats but other animals shepherded by humans in the city—parakeets, pythons, ferrets, raccoons, laboratory rats, fish in tanks. Police ride on huge horses and homeless men sit with squirrels on their shoulders. There may be more animals in the city than in the forest.

I first began to talk to Rose at our dog day. She always had her special brown dog on a leather leash, which looked as though she had cut it out herself. Rose was large and wore layers of clothes, loose jackets and shawls and aprons. She had a graceful way of walking, and as she moved, her layers wafting in the breeze, it almost looked as though she were floating. She often carried an easel or a few brushes in the hand not holding the leash.

Rose started talking about animals almost immediately. "Look at those pigeons over there!" she announced in her loud and strangely measured speech pattern. Her dog was patiently licking the heel of her shoe. "'Rats with wings,' everybody calls them," she continued. "Do you know their real name? Rock doves. They started living on the cliffs of the Mediterranean. Ancestors of rock doves were used by the ancient Hebrews as religious sacrifices." A wind wafted through her clothes, and she seemed to rise up like a kite. "Look at the feathers on their necks. Isn't it beautiful how the feathers shimmer in the light?"

Rose didn't stop for a moment. Her dog tried to lick my shoe, but I moved away. "Hear that chirping? Those are house sparrows." I began to realize that Rose didn't need any encouragement from me at all. She fed on the sound of her own words, and her voice gained more volume as she spoke. "The best time to watch sparrows is in a snowstorm. A snowstorm is the best time to go walking in this neighborhood anyway. When you see the city in the snow, you see that everything is in exactly the same place, but you *see* everything differently. You are *looking* at the city you know, but it is *not* the city you know. Everything is clean. It's like forgiveness, if only for a few hours. It's like God's mercy on every street."

Her dog reached again to lick my shoes. I shifted my feet and moved away from them both. "But more importantly," she continued, even more loudly, "the streets are absolutely, totally silent. This is so rare. You see, the snow seems to absorb all the sounds of the city."

Her dog circled and lay down with a resigned grunt. I shifted again and wanted to lie down too. "What does this have to do with sparrows?" I weakly volunteered.

Rose looked at me with intensity. "You'll find sparrows right in the middle of the snowstorm, cheeping and having fun. They are so small. They look weak and defenseless, but they are tough birds, survivors, New Yorkers with an attitude. You'll never get depressed after watching sparrows in a storm. They'll have all their feathers fluffed up in the snow, having as much fun as college kids on a beach at spring break."

I idly wondered when Rose, who lived in an abandoned building, had seen college kids on a beach. At that moment I had to leave to keep a dog that looked like a wolf from snapping a toy poodle in two at its tiny little waist. Dog day was a hit.

"Don't forget starlings," she said the next day, catching me in the park and pointing to some black birds. She spoke as if there were no break in the conversation from yesterday. "They whistle and squawk, but their language is highly complex. They have a sound for dog, cat, hawk, falcon, human armed, and human unarmed." I wanted to ask her how she knew this, but she was the type of person whose voice got louder every time you tried to put a word in edgewise.

Starlings and pigeons and sparrows now surrounded her as she threw out a handful of crumbs. Her shawl fluttered in the air like a queen's cape. She talked and cooed to the birds as if she were their mother. Her brown dog sat passively next to her, looking mournfully for something to lick. "For lots of older people, these are the only friends they have." I thought I saw a flicker of self-awareness as she glanced at me.

"Rats and squirrels are related," she surged ahead. "Rats take the night shift, and squirrels take the day shift. I think both mice and cats are cute but not to each other. Do you see the system in our neighborhood? There is a cat in every grocery store and restaurant here."

"I saw a rat in a diner last year," I broke in before she knew what was happening. "It ran right along the ledge used as a footrest under the counter. The rat ran right over the feet of the people sipping coffee. They never even knew it."

"What a brave rat," she said, which sounded rather odd to me. "I wonder why it had been thrust into such a dangerous situation in the middle of the day? Perhaps it was rejected from its community. I wonder why. Or maybe it was really really hungry." The conversation had become stranger and stranger to me. Rose's dog had found a piece of newspaper to lick.

Whenever I met her, Rose talked to me incessantly about animals. She stirred my interest about animals. She stirred my interest in spite of myself. Partially because of her discussions, I took a survival course.

One of the main points of the course was that in a wilderness situation, in order to survive, you must be able to look more closely at the things around you. We, as reluctant students, spent an afternoon lying on our stomachs in a meadow. Our assignment was to find the belly hair of a vole. I had little idea what a vole was, much less what its belly hair would look like. As I lay on the grass, I was thinking much more about chiggers and ticks. First, we had to find the little passageways in the grass that voles and other tiny animals use in a meadow. In all the times I walked through pasture land growing up, I never noticed these little trails. Once we began to notice these trails, with our eyes just a few inches from the ground, we began to look for the thinnest of tiny hairs.

No one in my group found one. Yet the time was not lost. As I lay on my stomach (feeling itchy) and looked at the miniature trails in front of me, every grain of dust became clear. It began to look like jewels. Then I noticed miniature, living things walking around the grains of dust that looked as big as boulders to them. Their bodies were about the size of a grain of dust, and they were brilliantly, strikingly red. Red as a sports car. As they picked their way upon this tiny trail, they were gorgeous.

I am not yet ready to lie on my stomach for an afternoon staring at a crack in the sidewalk on Seventh Street, but I am getting closer—actually, I'm not even ready to feed the starlings with Rose. Yet now I am drawn to even stranger species. Not only had the birds and the squirrels caught my attention; even the flies began to draw my admiration.

No science fiction, no fantasy, could draw from me anymore wonder than spending three minutes watching the common housefly as it wanders across a city trash can. Its structure for flight, its eyes, the movements of its head seem far more otherworldly than anything seen in a Hollywood film about aliens. There it is, even in the housefly, the fingerprints of our Maker.

My awareness of animals in the city began with a pit bull wearing a spiked collar on a sidewalk. My interest moved from a pit bull on the street to a dog day to Rose to a survival course to a housefly. Dogs and cats in the city may be at first a key to reaching out to other people, but they can become the passageway, a hidden door, to a whole web of living things that we have deemed invisible as we walk down the street. I am learning to walk even one block with new eyes. I am aware of an array of groups of living things, as complex as countries. Dogs, cats, squirrels, rats, mice, starlings, pigeons, sparrows, and flies become a United Nations of species relating and negotiating with us every time we step out the door. They reach out to us in the great dance of being alive on every street corner, begging us to see.

CHAPTER 10

Storefront Philosophy

*Then he said, "Do not come near; put off your shoes
from your feet, for the place on which you are standing
is holy ground."*

EXODUS 3:5 RSV

At the door of the house who will come knocking?
An open door, we enter
A closed door, a den
The world pulse beats beyond my door.

PIERRE ALBERT BIROT

THE SPACE IS SMALLER than a garage—about twenty feet by twenty feet. During previous times, I'm told, it was a porn shop, a social club, a pool hall, a candy store, a place for a motorcycle gang to keep its bikes. For the last twenty-five years or so it's been a storefront mission. Sometimes adults I don't know come in and say, "Wow! All the memories are coming back! I spent so much time here as a kid. Here's where the puppet shows were. Here's where they told the stories. Man, that was so long ago."

Places are important in the Bible. Places can be holy. One of the root meanings for the word *salvation* in the Hebrew is "to make a space for." If you doubt the power of a place, go back to your childhood home. Get down on your knees and crawl around. Memories will shoot through your body like an injection. Places where people pray a lot seem to have a quiet power, too, even if you enter those places for just a moment.

I heard a friend compare places to a frying pan. Some families have a favorite frying pan that makes pancakes better than any other. You don't want to scrub that pan too harshly because then you lose all the flavorful layers from all the great pancake breakfasts from the past. Perhaps places, emotionally, are like frying pans for us. They hold a faint hint of all the previous experiences that deepen and enrich our present experience there. In that sense, buildings have memories. They evoke remembrances we hardly know. Like fossils in a rock, remembrances that come from a place remind us of times that are far distant, when things were very different.

For me, the walls seem to absorb all the experiences that take place in a room. By looking hard in a place, we sometimes trace memories the way a tracker might see the evidence of some animal. The faintest hint of a track lies upon the surface.

After being here for many years, I could stand in that little storefront room and sense more than just the present. In a letter, Einstein once said, "The distinction between past, present and future is only an illusion, however persistent."[10] What a strange thing for a scientist to say.

Last week an adult I don't know very well started talking to me about the storefront: "We used to have Boy Scouts here. I loved that. Every person around me at that time was using or dealing drugs. I never got drunk or used drugs—I think Boy Scouts was one reason. It all happened here." Afterward, as I thought about this man, in a rare moment of quiet, I stood in the storefront, and past and future seemed to merge. Over there was where Bert grabbed Willie across the table in a purple rage and tried to choke him to death. Prying Bert's hands off Willie's neck was like loosening the grip of an alligator. Here is where Sandy was shooting up right in the middle of our church meal.

Over here was where a woman was sitting next to me during a Bible study. They had tried to find her a bra in the clothes closet earlier. All they could find was a short, loose-fitting blouse. She got tired in the middle of the Bible study and forgot and stretched her arms high into the air as she yawned. The bottom of her blouse lifted far higher than she imagined. I did not see her, but I knew something had happened as I looked at the grizzled, homeless men across from me in the circle. They looked at each other to see if they had hallucinated. They could not quite believe what they had just seen next to the mission pastor in the middle of a Bible study in this little storefront.

Over there was where an angry teenager threw a heavy chair across the room and broke a table. Here is where I stood next to the broken table. Anger and fear roared through my nervous system, urging me both to strike out and to hold back. It was like flooring the gas pedal and slamming on the brakes at the same time. Over there is where I stood, hundreds of times, to say a prayer for our meals, when everyone is invited and no one is turned away (unless you try to choke someone or toss heavy furniture). Up in that corner, behind the Sheetrock is where we put a kazoo, of all things. It's there to remember Louie, a former murderer, pimp, and crack addict who came to the Lord and loved to play Christian songs on his kazoo. Here is where Ellen had a seizure on the floor in the middle of a meal. Over there is where Gus, on a freezing day when you could see your breath inside the storefront, announced, "I want to be born again. But I want to be born again in Florida." This is where we divided the space in half and started a church with its own Sunday school.

Since it is a church in a storefront, like thousands of churches in storefronts in inner cities all over the country, there are many memories of God's saving work. Here is where Sammy asked Christ into his life. He didn't know much and was surprised when he stole a three-wheeler the next day and was rebuked for it. Here is where Brad accepted the Lord and stopped using heroin. There is where we put his picture during his memorial service after he died of AIDS. Next to the sink is where Josie prayed and asked Christ into her life. Over there is where Will stood, with his head bowed, rededicated his life to Christ, and stopped using crack. In this tiny space over all the years, hundreds of people have accepted the Lord or rededicated their lives. The memories are bittersweet. Some of the people have returned to their families or to a better life; some are dead.

As I stood in that room, thousands of memories rushed in all at once. I read a fanciful story once about where people came for the Final Judgment. God had to remain quiet most of the time, because He knew everything about everything. He knew what had happened to that marble you lost when you were nine years old and how long it stayed in the gutter. He knew when it was moved by a heavy rain and how far, why a squirrel put it in its nest, how the second baby squirrel in her second litter chipped its tooth on it, and on and on. It was simply too much information for the others in the court. I suppose forgetting is a tremendous gift. Our minds simply cannot handle all that goes on, even in one tiny room.

What will people remember in a few decades about us in New York City? Perhaps something former Mayor Rudolph Giuliani said or baseball player Derek Jeter did. But the vast majority of people and experiences will pass on. A few people who knew us will remember a few things, and then in a few more decades, the memories will be all gone. From an earthly view, our experiences are written in water.

The storefronts will last a few more decades than we do, perhaps. Little storefront churches played a noble part in the cities during the 1970s and 1980s. When many people, businesses, and institutions were abandoning the inner city, the little storefront churches kept hanging on. With a handful of people and limited space and a poorly painted sign, they kept on when sociologists and theologians called the inner-city crisis hopeless. They had few rich members and few big buildings. Yet they stayed and provided friendship, prayer, and true life for many children and adults. Some of these people were caught in a dark trinity of poverty, drugs, and illiteracy, yet these storefront churches seemed to understand. As the cities were reviving and moving to a new stage, these little storefronts were like the poor wise man described in Ecclesiastes: "There was a little city with few men in it; and a great king came against it and besieged it, building great siegeworks against it. But there was found in it a poor wise man, and he by his wisdom delivered the city. Yet no one remembered that poor man" (9:14–15 RSV).

Many little neighborhoods in the city were besieged by satanic forces that tried to rule those areas, and these small churches held the line. Yet now, in the flush of reinvestment and new people with more money, these little pockets of healing may be forgotten.

Storefront churches come and go. So do storefront businesses. One evening, I left our storefront church and walked down the street. Stopping by a small clothing store, I looked over at the window. Because of the streetlight behind me, all I saw was my own reflection. I patted the back of my head where some hair was sticking up. As I continued to look at my reflection, without moving, something happened. Somehow, my eyes stopped looking at myself. In an instant the whole world of the clothing store inside became visible—colorful clothes on display, a salesperson in the background talking to a customer, posters on the wall. Although looking at the same window, I saw something totally different from what I had seen a moment before.

If we were to see truly any one of these little storefronts, it would take many lifetimes. Walking down the streets, we see businesses in the first glow of starting out with all their plans and dreams. We see other businesses and churches thriving. Still others are on their last legs, vainly holding on to life, before the storefront is dark again, the electricity is turned off, and the For Rent sign is put on its door.

The row of storefronts on many streets is like a row of different flowers, each blooming for a short while, then each dying at different times and waiting for the next growth. It is a drama that continues incessantly like the seasons, sweeping up people's hopes and sweat and heartbreak, yet we walk by and never even notice. To see these places requires more wisdom in the streets than we can muster.

CHAPTER 11

Something More Concrete

And the street of the city was pure gold,
transparent as glass.

REVELATION 21:21B RSV

Whoever does not believe in miracles is not a realist.

DAVID BEN GURION

IT'S ONE THING TO SEE WHAT'S *on* the street; it's another thing to look *at* it. As a fish never notices the water it is in, the city person never notices the cement.

The cement of the city is a great blessing, I suppose, a protection from mud. As bipeds, we "pound the pavement" with our two lower extremities. Where I live, we play football and baseball on cement. Grass is a precious commodity that's fenced off. You walk by it and look at it as if in a museum.

Above all, the cement of the streets is hard. It is a reminder of the cracked heads, chipped teeth, and bloody hands of those who come in contact with it too suddenly. Cement is what makes the metaphor of "the streets" so perfect in describing the harsh difficulties of life. Actually *falling* out of a window is not what hurts; it's *hitting* the pavement that creates the problems. Sooner or later, the person who is drifting will face the hard reality of the street. It is as sure as the law of gravity.

The street person knows better than anyone else the literal hardness of the street. The sidewalk is that person's bed. Young business people may complain about getting shinsplints while jogging for exercise on the sidewalk, but the street people have to grind their faces in it every night. They know the reality of making cardboard into a pillow, of curling up so that their hips and shoulders don't ache from this hardest of beds, of stuffing newspaper under their clothing in order to stay warm.

She called herself Fresca. One of the people at our church met her at a place where clean needles are handed out to heroin addicts. After months, our ministry worker convinced Fresca to come to a meal at our church.

Fresca had fifteen necklaces on. She came in with her head bowed down, as if she were some medieval serf in the presence of people far better than she felt she was. Her hands were puffy and dirty; she wore many layers of clothing. She made eye contact with no one.

"This is my friend, Fresca." We were introduced, and Fresca held out a limp swollen hand for me to shake. "Hello," she whispered and tilted her head sideways to look up at me for the briefest of moments.

After that, from time to time, Fresca began to try to attend some of our meetings. Sometimes she told me, "I tried to come yesterday, but I only got up to the door. I stood on the sidewalk for about a half hour. I kept thinking that I am not worthy to come in."

If Fresca did get the courage to come in, she would hunch over in her chair, with her head down, her necklaces dangling to her knees. Sometimes she would have what I call "the droops," sitting or standing motionless for long periods of time with her eyes closed. She said she was not using drugs, but such motionless behavior was common for those who are shooting up. Slowly, as we got to know her, we learned more of her story of growing up very dependent on her mother, losing her mother, going to prison, being let out of prison, and having nowhere to go.

"The guards kept telling me to go on, to go on. But I just stood there at the bus stop outside the prison. I was scared because I had nowhere to go. I let the buses pass and hoped they would let me back inside the prison. I had no idea what to do."

Her life had drifted to heroin and finally to living on the streets. "I must really be a bad person. I have my little cart of stuff I keep behind a building. Now that the police won't let you sleep anywhere, you really have to be smart. You have to sneak around and hide and have some friends who will help you. The street is such a hard place to live. Sometimes I stay up all night as I lie on the sidewalk. I've gotten used to how hard it is, but I'm scared someone's going to mess with me. Every night I feel terror.

"People can be pretty rough. Sometimes they won't let me come in and get a cup of coffee because I have no place to take a shower. Last week someone didn't want me sleeping on the sidewalk in front of their building. They poured hot water on me from a second story window. You know, they could have just talked to me."

Fresca's bedroom was a cement sidewalk. She was on the run from many things, both inside and outside. Her sense of total unworthiness made it hard for her to hear that God loved her. Just as she stood outside the church building, she was convinced that if there was a heaven, she would stand outside it forever. Perhaps someone might even pour hot water on her from heaven's gate to let her know she was not welcome.

"The people at this church are so gentle," Fresca said. "They hold my hand; they pray with me. They joke with me and make me laugh." Fresca still slept on the sidewalk for her own reasons, but sometimes she would sleep in the apartment of one of the people in our church.

Slowly, like ice thawing on a sidewalk, she warmed up to the realization that God loved her even while she was a sinner. She agreed with God that she had done wrong (no problem there), prayed for Christ to come into her life, and turned away from sin. She prayed this prayer quietly, bent over, sitting on a folding chair in the corner of the church.

Inch by inch, step by step, things began to change. It was the furthest thing from something dramatic. It was like the coming of spring. Nothing changed hour by hour, but month after month showed that something new was happening.

Fresca still slept on cement. But she gained confidence at church and would share her story. She laughed more. Eventually she even led Bible studies. She entered an outpatient drug rehabilitation program. She contacted her family. It was a long, long process. The slow growth was punctuated by vivid insights for her.

One of the places our church meets is in a basement. The doors are blocked by huge boards, so that if someone breaks into the basement, he can't go up into the rest of the building. The frames of some doors have holes in them, where rats have gnawed a passageway.

One day Fresca was going to the rest room after worship was over. The person locking up didn't know she was still there and locked her in. Fresca turned off the light, rushed out of the rest room, and found herself in total darkness, locked in the basement, with no one in the entire building. She screamed. No answer. She groped for any kind of light. She didn't know where she was. It was like being in a cave.

She frantically felt along the walls of the basement, trying to find a way out. She found a door. The doorknob was not locked. She didn't know that it was a Dutch door that led into a place for children. The bottom part of the door was unlocked. The top part was not. She held the doorknob, pushed open the bottom half, and rushed into the room, hoping that it was the way out. The top part of the door wouldn't give, slamming the upper part of her body down to the concrete floor as her legs went out from under her. There she was, face up on the cement of this old basement, looking into pitch darkness. She remembered the rats.

"I'm not going to give up," she told herself. She picked herself up and wandered, with her hands outstretched, in the darkness for a long time. Her head hit an old water pipe and almost knocked her down again. Finally, she told herself, standing in the darkness, "All right, I am trapped. I can't see and I can find absolutely no way to get out. I am going to pray."

She slowly bent down on her knees in the darkness. Little bits of gravel from the cement of the basement floor made imprints on her jeans and on her skin. Yet at the moment she kneeled to pray, something happened. Her perspective was lowered just enough, that she could see the light beneath the door in the far back that led to some stairs to the outside.

With that new perspective, she made her way toward the light and unbarred the doors. She was free.

"Prayer made the difference," she proudly told us later. "When I stood, all I saw was darkness, but kneeling to pray gave me the little change of perspective so that I could see."

Fresca eventually found a place to live besides the sidewalk. It was a long way away from us. We didn't see her much after that. She had some trouble and she moved to another place, even farther away. I haven't seen her for a long time. I don't know where she is now. My calendar tells me that tomorrow is her birthday.

Fresca knew the streets in a way I never will. For her, the sidewalk was like the bank of a river. The roadway itself was the place where all the cars, like huge fish floating in carbon monoxide, glided past her day by day. She didn't know what the story was for the people in the cars, and they didn't know her story. The people in the cars were always separated by tires, springs, metal, and glass from that hard surface, the surface that kissed her face each night. Yet, to me, the people in the cars were the ones none the wiser. Because they made sure their knees never touched the concrete, I think it was a little harder for them to see the light.

CHAPTER 12

A World of Barriers

[Jesus] has united us by breaking down the wall of hatred that separated us.

EPHESIANS 2:14 CEV

Something there is that doesn't love a wall.

ROBERT FROST, "MENDING WALL"

IT TOOK SO LONG TO GET TO HIM. I'd been with him at the funeral of his stepfather when he was barely a teenager. I hadn't seen him for a long time. Now he was at one of our city's most famous prisons.

It took all day, just to see him, even though he was in my city. First I took a subway, studying the map. Then a bus to the first line of defense for the jail. Checkpoints. Family members loaded up on another bus to go across the bridge to the island. Single file through more procedures. Forms to fill out. A huge waiting room with mothers and children. A TV was blaring, fans droning. More waiting. My sweaty shirt stuck to the back of the chair as I shifted around in my seat.

Now that we were inside the first line of enclosures, we waited a long time and were finally called and directed to another bus. It was an old school bus with torn seat cushions. We drove among the bleak blockhouses. Everything seemed gray and metallic. Mothers and girlfriends and brothers looked out the windows as if this were all routine.

In the particular blockhouse that was our destination, we were screened again and required to remove belts and anything else that might be suspicious. We could see razor wire out the window. More corridors, more walls, more double doors. Our hands were stamped and names taken once again.

Finally, we were led into a huge room, with tables set out like a school cafeteria. The air became charged with expectancy. We all sat down with the realization that soon sitting across from us would be the person we had taken so much time to visit. Apparently this part of the prison was for young men, perhaps first-time offenders, so they didn't have to sit behind a screen.

I was having feelings I didn't think I'd be having. I was nervous and felt out of my element. That nervousness didn't really surprise me. As I looked around the room I replayed the tapes of society in my mind. Here were the families of criminals, the angry underclass. It should feel like one of the visiting scenes in a second-rate movie, all dead serious, filled with anger for incarceration, whether the confinement was done justly or unjustly. These were dangerous people and questionable families, drug dealers, thieves, people not afraid to use violence.

Yet there was no somberness or seriousness at all. It looked like a holiday, like the last day of summer camp when parents come to pick up their kids. Brothers, sisters, and girlfriends could not stay in their seats. They chattered like squirrels. Mothers sat back and clutched their hands to their hearts.

Slowly, one or two at a time, the prisoners entered the room. They could hardly keep from running. Families squealed. No matter how hard the prisoners tried, they could not act tough or look mature. They looked like what they were, young kids excited that someone had come to see them.

In barrier after barrier, enclosure after enclosure, in this drab cell block in the middle of a hot summer in a hot city, it was Christmas morning.

Finally, the young man I came to visit appeared. His name was Bud. He tried to look uninterested, but he was very pleased. He sauntered over, going as slowly as he could, trying to look cool. "What's up?" he said. "Oh that?" He turned his head, as I looked at a crude tattoo on his arm. "I did that with a safety pin, 'cause I didn't have anything else to do here." A few uneven numbers, probably some code, checkered his pocked arm.

As he talked, I thought Bud's heart seemed pierced and pocked too. The walls seemed to make his self-hatred worse. We talked on about other little things. But for that time, things had changed between us. There was an unspeakable bond that we didn't have to talk about. It was a bond that no walls could separate and perhaps the walls had helped to create.

As I went home that day, as I reversed the tedious process of checkpoints and waiting rooms, I was never quite the same. As I rode on the bus away from the prison, I saw every chain-link fence, every circle of razor wire, every wall and lock, all the metal bars on all the windows, all the metal roll-down shutters on all the store windows.

This is the reality of the fallen city. When my family and I moved into a ground-floor apartment, there were strong metal bars across nearly every window and a metal gate with a lock covering our back door. The previous tenant had had some robberies. I was the same as everyone else. The first thing I did was make sure the remaining open spaces at the top of the windows were covered with bars too.

I thought about my own memories as I rode away from the prison on that summer day. I saw the whole city as a mirror of the process of enclosure on the island. Just as on the island every measure was taken to keep people in, conversely, in the city, every possible measure was taken to keep people out. These measures appeared in every single cubicle and living unit, no matter how small, piled up one on top of the other in a staggering number of components.

This reality is part of what I see when I walk the streets now. Window gates, iron bars, razor wire, bricked-up entrances.

I wish I could tell you that the bond with Bud lasted, but it didn't. Later he stalked his own mother until she locked herself in a bathroom in one of our meetings. He knocked me aside and slapped the telephone out of my hand when I called for help.

After his mother died, on a hot summer day in the park, this same man, now grown, threatened to kill me when I refused to give him her remaining public assistance checks. He flexed his muscles and thrust his face up to mine in total fury. "Choose your words carefully," I told him. "They may have legal implications."

In a boiling, insolent rage, he said, "I will do anything necessary to keep you from attending my mother's funeral service at the church across town." Then he turned around and stomped off across the park. Not a great lover of confrontations, I wilted onto a park bench after he disappeared. As the service approached, a long-time neighbor told me that my young "friend," who by now had a long list of arrests due to violence, had told her something.

"Bud says he's paid ten dollars to a couple of junkies to beat you up if you came near the funeral service." After a storm of fear swept over me, my next emotion was hurt pride. The cost of my own demise seemed kind of bargain-basement at ten dollars.

Never being much of a streetwise person anyway, I walked alone rather gingerly to the funeral service. I took a circuitous route. I looked over my shoulder far more often than I meant to. Funny noises made me jump like a deer. When I first began working at our mission, I had seen the results of what a couple of guys with baseball bats or iron bars could do to a person. I didn't want to see those results again.

As I entered the church, my reverent silence was more strategic planning at where to sit. I remembered that Wyatt Earp always tried to sit with his back to a wall. A wall, a wall, my kingdom for a wall. No such place here, unless I pretended to be an usher.

I finally sat next to the aisle, midway toward the front. I wondered how unnatural it looked when I casually craned my neck around to keep the back door in the corner of my eye. I tilted my head to the side like a chicken. Could I possibly sit like this through the entire service and look even vaguely respectful? What would it feel like to have a bat make connection with my skull as I read the words of remembrance in the bulletin? Would I hear the crack of its impact?

Believe me, in my scared heart, beating as fast as a rabbit's, I wanted as many barriers as possible between me and harm's way. Bring them on. On the other hand, I wasn't going to be walled out of my friend's funeral service by her son's violent promise.

Nothing happened in the service. After all the threats, Bud didn't even show up himself. My vivid imagination had once again dragged me to a bad neighborhood of the mind, far removed from any reality.

I don't know if the story is over with this gentleman. I do know that something in us hates barriers, and yet, sadly, we need them. Even though Bud is roaming free somewhere, he's still locked in a prison of anger, and others who come in contact with him need to be protected from his violence.

The city is a maze of walls, seen and unseen. Many of these ethnic, political, and economic barriers bring lifelessness for those on both sides. The Bible sees Christ's selfless, self-giving death as the crumbling of the walls between the tribalism of its own context, the racial difference between Jews and Gentiles (Eph. 2:14). How can we put on the love of Christ to see the real, intractable, seemingly irreconcilable differences in the cities of our times from Jerusalem to Belfast to Kosovo to Kabul to Baghdad to New York? The cost seems so high.

For a year in the 1970s I lived two blocks from the Berlin Wall, I was told if I took a stroll in the park and came too close to the wall, the soldier in the tower would give me one warning and then he would shoot me. These instructions put a bit of a damper on my first tentative walks in the park. In all the conversations I had with residents of the city through an entire year, not one person ever even mentioned the possibility that the wall would come down. The wall was simply assumed, eternal, immutable. The news in the late eighties seemed almost magical to me. It was wondrous to watch civilians standing on the wall I lived so close to. It was a sign that many things assumed to be absolutely hopeless in the city may not be, after all.

According to the last book of the Bible, there is a high and thick wall around our future city (Rev. 21:12). And even though the unworthy are outside, the gates are always open (Rev. 21:25). Always. Someday our new home in the city will have the balance of welcoming and protection that our cities have never been quite able to find as we walk the streets now, for we are less wise and more fearful city dwellers than we will be in times to come.

CHAPTER 13

The Flood of Information

*These sayings come from God, our only shepherd,
and they are like nails that fasten things together.
My child, I warn you to stay away from any
teaching except these. There is no end to books,
and too much study will wear you out.*

ECCLESIASTES 12:11B–12 CEV

*But people have a right not to know, and it is a more
valuable one—the right not to have their divine souls*

stuffed with gossip, nonsense, vain talk. A person who works and leads a meaningful life has no need for this excessive and burdening flow of information.

ALEKSANDR SOLZHENITSYN,
COMMENCEMENT ADDRESS
HARVARD, JUNE 8, 1978

THE TRASH HEAP SMELLED. On it were an old computer and a dirty monitor. No one picked them up. They looked like tombstones. As I looked at the computer, I imagined the excitement when the owner first pulled it out of its box, with the smell of fresh plastic and Styrofoam. I imagined the thrill as he checked out the CD encyclopedia for the first time and when he made connections on the Internet. Perhaps he cried as he saw a movie on the screen or whiled away boring hours as he played video games he downloaded from friends.

Giving and receiving information is the passion of our species. We can't keep ourselves from communicating. Thousands and thousands of cell phones, Internet connections, fax machines, radios, cable TVs, headphones, and intercoms each instant in the city are churning at hyperspeed. Each moment on the street is hypercharged as electronic devices blast out and catch data. Yet if such seemingly infinite possibilities are all that we have, that cracked computer on the garbage dump could serve as an apt tombstone for our lives.

After his long imprisonment and detention in the former USSR, Aleksandr Solzhenitsyn made a remarkable commencement address at Harvard. Having endured oppression in a totalitarian state for his writings, Solzhenitsyn acknowledged our acute right to know, something for which he had paid such a high personal price. But he was also an astute observer of our own society in the West. How astonishing it was that he also said we have the right not to know, to be protected from the endless flow of gossip and superficial information which engulfs us.[11]

LONLINESS

TENSION

GRIEF

INTEGRATION

This huge river of information that floods our senses each moment can become a distraction. Centuries ago, Pascal, the mathematician, reminded us that most people don't want to think about the most important question of life: What happens when we die? If there is even the remotest possibility of eternal life (or eternal damnation), we would surely want to explore those options before we do things that would affect the few decades that we live on earth. But apparently we don't want to think about that question. If a huge crowd were asked that question, many would say something like this: "I never really thought about it much." We move through life as if enchanted. We are caught up with what Pascal calls "diversions"—being extravagantly concerned about the minutest details of secondary concerns, such as racing, or the theater.[12]

Now, hundreds of years after his comments, the opportunity for diversions has gone wild. Recently former President Bill Clinton spoke to a local high school graduation. He gave an example to show how much the world has changed. He said, "In 1992, when I began to serve as president, there were only fifty Web sites in existence. In 2000, when I left office, there were over 350 million Web sites."[13]

We live and move in a vastly concentrated invisible web of diversions. These confront us with seemingly endless possibilities for distraction each moment. Aldous Huxley, the twentieth-century intellectual who was no apparent fan of Christianity, once said, "Society should be judged by the extent to which it makes meditation possible."[14] By Huxley's standards, our society has flunked. With our abundance of noisemakers and word carriers, we have not made meditation, or I would say prayer, easy, especially in the churning city.

Followers of Christ sometimes seem to be little specks desperately trying to paddle upstream against an ever-widening torrent of distractions. Albert Schweitzer, the unorthodox Bible scholar and Bach expert who served as a doctor in Africa, was aware of the distractions that even the best of culture provided. He believed in taking the time to think deeply about things, to avoid simply being a technician, and be involved in what he called "elemental thinking." He said that if each person, when part of a funeral procession, would take only three minutes to truly think about the mystery of death and life, the world would be different.[15]

No wonder in this sea of distractions and superficial information people in general feel a sense of lostness. This experience may explain some of the frenzy you sense as you walk the streets, as people scurry from sensory experience to sensory experience, from bar to concert to movie to sports event, trying to find some meaning in places that can never really provide it.

I get lost in it too. These possibilities are global, but in the heart of the city, with people, electronics, radio, and TV air waves reverberating in density, the invisible skein of information and possibilities seem almost tangible.

On one street corner on a normal day, I can hear rap booming from a Jeep at the curbside and salsa from a tenement building's window above me. I see the news blaring on a TV at a fruit stand. I pass a store selling Tibetan clothing and philosophy books. Next to it is a store advertising psychic readings for five dollars. Next to it is a bookstore selling what it claims are politically revolutionary books. A man hands me a flyer that says, "Give me that old time religion—Witchcraft." Down the street I can smell the incense outside the mosque from a man selling his wares on a folding table. The cultural compression and the proliferation of choices create a tidal wave of distractions for each step on the sidewalk.

Each day we carry the most pressing news events from across the globe in our minds. We are faced with worldviews from every culture and are aware of hardships on every continent. Sometimes the information is empowering, but, in truth, we bear the sorrows of the world each day in a way that the nomad Abraham three thousand years before us never knew. No wonder we sometimes feel we have lost our way.

Thank God that in the city we have a clear and living reference point—Jesus Christ. The Bible says that of the making of books (and magazines, movies, TV shows, radio programs, and web sites) there is no end. Sometimes at night a streetlight in the park will reflect off all the leaves on the surrounding trees and make the leaves look as though they have taken on a perfect circular symmetry around the light. This is what Jesus Christ does to all the chaotic choices with which we are bombarded. His presence brings order. His guidance is clear. Choosing Christ's path of love gives clarity in the barrage of choices we face each day.

Merely serving a current of information, merely chasing after it, will make us as dead as that stained computer on the garbage dump. The Bible says that Jesus is the "exact representation" of God (Heb. 1:3 TEV). The self-giving love of Christ is the heart of God. Knowing the great self-giver guides me as I listen to the possibilities of the streets. Christ saves me from the flow of diversions. He makes me streetwise in spite of myself. A torrent of diversions and information engulf every street of the city. Through Christ, God still saves us from the flood.

CHAPTER 14

Money Makes the World Go 'Round

You cannot serve both God and money.

MATTHEW 6:24B TEV

There are three conversions necessary: the conversion of the heart, mind, and purse.

MARTIN LUTHER

I COULD HAVE BEEN AT A motivational conference. It was the same tone. "Sharon taught me everything I know about confidence," Gary told me. I squinted my eyes as I tried to understand what he was talking about. The day was gray and cold. We were standing on a street corner. "She took me under her wing and trained me," Gary continued as he looked up and down the street. He put a gloved hand up to his mouth and coughed. The gloves had holes. "She showed me how not to be afraid when I asked for money. She told me to just do it, look up and ask for money. If someone shouted back 'Get a job!' I wasn't supposed to let that get to me. I would have never survived on the street if she hadn't taught me. Sharon gave me the confidence to beg," Gary announced proudly.

I winced again as I tried to see Gary's world, which seemed to me turned inside out. "Wouldn't you rather have the confidence to work?" I started to say. Instead, I kept quiet and tried to understand what Gary was telling me.

"I was so shy and scared before I met Sharon," Gary continued. "Sharon built me up. She showed me I didn't have to care what others say to me. I remember sitting on the sidewalk with my hat in front of me and that first guy who walked past. I was so nervous. I couldn't look up. I just mumbled something into my hands. Sharon didn't give up. By the second day, I was making ten to twenty bucks in a couple of hours. Sharon showed me how to say, 'Thank you,' and 'God bless you, sir,' no matter how mean the person was to me. You never know when they might come back and change their mind. Sharon was the best thing that ever happened to me in the city. Without her, I'd be lower than nothing, I'd be . . ."

"What's lower than a street beggar?" my "parent" voice wanted to ask.

"Dead," Gary continued and coughed in his shredded gloves again.

I stood with him on the corner and contemplated his success story.

A beggar's money in the street is the tip of the iceberg for a vast system of values that seems to make the city run. Conventional beggar wisdom must dictate that a visible dollar and some coins in a hat or a can will draw more money to the same location. Begging fads and styles change on the street—signs, pet dogs, children, crutches, backpacks. All tell a story to draw money from the passerby. Yet, a little bit of money in the cup is always part of the stage.

There's something in me that hates the beggars and the one-way flow of cash on the street. Yet I don't want to think about the issue too much, because I, too, receive money because of the generosity of others. If we think about it a little more, we all receive gifts that are beyond our ability to repay, no matter who we are. When I criticize a beggar, I don't want to be reminded that everything I offer was given to me by God. His one-way flow of shocking generosity puts us all in the same boat. There are two words for *poor* used in the New Testament. One word means living in poverty, just barely making it. The other word means absolutely destitute. Without the help of someone else, this desperate person will die. Guess which word Jesus used when He said, "Blessed are the poor in Spirit."

Please don't put me in the category with Gary. There's something in me that doesn't want to be a beggar in Spirit. The money Gary puts in his hat as he plies his trade is the green symbol for the hopes and fears of the worldly city, especially New York City.

On the same street corner with Gary begging, I can sometimes see another handful of bills change hands. The small-time drug dealer stands to the side and looks purposeful. He seems as energetic and focused as a Wall Street investor. He walks down the street a bit with his client. They touch hands in a businesslike manner. I can see the flash of money or a bag as they part ways. At times, the dealer may peel from his pocket a whole roll of money, bill layered upon bill in a wad the size of an apple. All exchanges are made quickly, and the dealer keeps moving.

Of course, money comes out at the newsstands and drink counters that face the street, the outward sign of money on the surface that intimates the thousands of exchanges of money inside every store, restaurant, and office.

Money is like a knife. It can be used for good or for ill. It can cut bread for a neighbor or stab a friend in the back. Every few months a man comes by as I stand out in the street talking to people on Wednesday night. We have a meal open to anyone who wants to come. The man grabs my hand and presses a crumpled twenty-dollar bill into it. I don't know his name. Apparently he got a meal here once or twice, many years ago, and now he's doing fine. I guess it's a practical thank-you to God that he's better. He always makes the relay to me quickly; he doesn't want to talk about it.

Money has its own journey and story on the street. It is too complex. Only God could tell that story. One time we found a huge bucket of coins on the front step of the storefront. It took two people to lug it in because it was so heavy. It turned out to be about four hundred dollars worth of nickels, pennies, and dimes, which we turned into services for others.

Jesus always had a cavalier attitude toward money, or so it seems to me. If money wasn't provided by a group of ladies (Luke 8:3), it was provided by a fish (Matt. 17:27). He had a "garden" mentality about money, whereas I often have a "desert" mentality. He saw the plenty; I see the lack.

These issues are not theoretical for us in the ministry in our neighborhood. As the Lord provided more jobs, food, and tutoring through our ministry, the realization of the monthly payroll became more acute for me. Slow learner that I am, it still takes me a while to "step over the log" of focusing on our own lack to rest in Christ's abundance. I remember realizing we had to pay twice as much for an insurance premium than I thought. It would wipe out our account. I took the step over the log. "We've got to pay this premium. It's the right thing to do. Make out the check please so we can mail it today." An hour later, a check arrived in the mail for twice the amount of the premium. As I held the letter with the check inside, a Scripture verse came to mind: "Before they call, I will answer; and while they are yet speaking, I will hear" (Isa. 65:24 KJV). Several months later we had $1.78 in the bank and seventeen people on our payroll. God had provided month by month in amazing ways for us through gifts from people and grants we had applied for. I looked at my coworker and said, "I have no idea how we will get through the fall. All the normal channels of giving for our programs have already given. I don't have a clue." Perhaps, for that moment, I was where God wanted to get me. The next month an unexpected series of gifts, out of the blue, provided for us far more than I could imagine.

Like information, money flows through the streets in invisible channels. I have heard perhaps a hundred stories from street people that go something like this: "I had no money at all and I didn't know where to turn. I prayed to God for help, and I turned around, and there, next to the trash can, was a ten-dollar bill. Can you believe it? Just when I needed it. I was able to get breakfast for myself and my friend."

These stories are told again and again. They are held close to the heart by those who have very little else except an open dependence on God.

Here are the two dangers for me concerning money. The first is that money encourages us to see everything as a fee for service. At the end of the Book of Revelation, there is a woman who symbolizes the great city that has dominion over the powers of the earth (chap. 17). She is a prostitute. Surely she is much more in the vision, but she is nothing less than a symbol of a whole payment mentality.

In our mission Bible study, when we looked at this chapter, a man said, "Yeah, the man pays a fee for a service that satisfies his lust. You pay some money, and you get about twenty minutes." He paused, since he was in a Bible study, to consider the truth of his statement. He continued earnestly, "Sometimes, you're lucky if you get five minutes!" He looked down quickly at his Bible, realizing he had disclosed more than he had intended. In the Bible, sure enough, it is the merchants who weep when this city system falls (Rev. 18:11–19).

In the final chapters of the Bible, the new city is also envisioned as a woman. But this time she is a bride (Rev. 21). The attitude of the bride and groom is the opposite of the customer and a prostitute. The bride and groom want to give everything for each other. It is a relationship of love rather than a system of fees. The theme of the Bible is consistent at the end. In the city, God wants companionship; we tend to focus on results and payment.[16] So the first danger of money is that focusing on it in this life tends to bleed into the way we see everything.

For me, the second danger concerning money is this: Money can create the illusion that we are making progress. I can look back and say, "I have saved more money than previously. I have a bigger house. I have more clothing. I can buy more things." This mentality puts up a false goal post so that we can look back with a false satisfaction in our lives. We forget to look over the years and see if we have grown in trusting God, in generosity of spirit, in humility, in real care for others. The person thankful for finding ten dollars on the street may have a heart the size of the sky. The successful, middle-aged property owner may have a soul the size of a peanut. Or vice versa. Just when I develop a nice comfortable prejudice against money, God brings to me the incredibly generous businessman and the self-serving street person who is a leech. "A leech has two daughters, and both are named 'Give me!'" (Prov. 30:15 TEV).

As I looked at Gary's hat on the street, I saw money. As I grew as a city dweller, sometimes I began to see the flow of money in invisible channels. I live twenty blocks from Wall Street, which channels rivers of money and is the keeper of a vast reservoir of wealth. Yet the children I work with, so close to so much, sometimes can't read. Their classrooms sometimes don't have enough textbooks. Not too far from Wall Street, working mothers wait in long lines for used children's clothes to stretch their budgets. Blocks away from wealthy investors, sweatshops employ foreign workers at subpoverty wages. Political categories come and go, but a basic Bible concept is hard to stamp out. God, through Amos, showed His great concern for the inequity of the flow of resources. For example, Amos addressed the women who unthinkingly lived in luxury while others were oppressed. He called them fat cows (Amos 4:1). Hardly politically correct. Amos pointed out that those who lay on fancy beds and drank wine in bowls, rather than cups, had a marked lack of awareness of what was happening around them. There would be consequences (Amos 6:4–7).

As I began to be aware of the way money works in the city, I kept thinking about a conversation I had in the mid-1970s with a German family who lived very close to Dachau. Dachau was a concentration camp that brutalized Jews and others during World War II and used ovens to eliminate all the dead bodies that piled up.

"We never knew those terrible things were going on at Dachau," the family told me. "We knew there were people working there, but we had no idea. How awful to think these things were happening right before our eyes, and we didn't see it."

This was a family of honest, frugal farmers with Christian ideals who worked faithfully through the World War II era. If the reality of what was happening right next door to them was thrust in their faces, surely they would have taken action. But they didn't take the time to know. They had a blind spot.

As I thought about money, I wondered what the blind spot of my generation would be. I wondered if, thirty years from now, I would look back on the vast inequities of money, the deep poverty next to embarrassing wealth, and say, "How awful to think these things were happening right before my eyes." Am I the rich man who never noticed Lazarus crying at his gate (Luke 16:19–31)?

"There's more in the Bible about money and finances than there is about prayer," growled one surly Bible scholar on the street. I'm not sure about that. But I do know from the Bible that God passionately cares about people, and money affects people. The invisible channels of money crisscross the city from the mightiest rivers to the tiniest trickles. As we walk the streets, we cannot ignore these rivulets and Amazons. Forgetting the tiny trickles is a mistake.

"If Christians exclude those who are poor in the city, they may find themselves excluding Christ," I was informed by the same street theologian. If we can't see this, perhaps God might put us in a place where we can understand this—sitting on the sidewalk next to Gary for a while with a dollar bill in our hat in front of us.

Reflection: Jesus

The Pusher
Luke 23:24

He wasn't born in a great place, and in the beginning, He was on the verge of being homeless. Even as a baby, people were trying to kill Him, and His family had to cross borders and become refugees just to stay alive. Later, there were rumors in His village about who His father was, and the kids must have teased Him a lot. But somehow He pushed on through that childhood time.

As a young man there were also lonely times, temptations about His calling when no one was around, and people who thought He was crazy. Even His family thought He was crazy (Mark 3:21). Perhaps that's one reason He had such a heart for those with unsettled minds. As He pushed out sickness and fakeness, times became hot and uncertain. Forces started coming together that might suddenly rub Him out. Yet still He pushed toward the goal.

Going to Jerusalem for Him was as safe as putting one's head in an oven. It was like walking on a minefield among people who could be either friends or enemies or both. On that last night, He saw it all closing in on Him. Then He had to push Himself just to keep from quitting.

In the end they did rub Him out, pinned Him to some boards like an insect, made sure He faced the ultimate barrier, the final resistance, the impassable wall—death. And yet, in some unutter-able way of God, He pushed on through.

You might think that on the other side of death Jesus would push back some retribution, some consequences, some justice upon all those people who did such things to Him. But not really. He wasn't that kind of pusher.

Street Vision

(SEEING THE POWER OF GOD'S
MENDING WORK IN THE CHRONIC AND
SUDDEN TRAUMAS OF THE CITY)

CHAPTER 15

Counting
the Towers

People of God, walk around Zion and count the towers.
PSALM 48:12 TEV

*Our concern is not how to worship in the catacombs, but
rather how to remain human in the skyscrapers.*
ABRAHAM JOSHUA HESCHEL

I'VE HEARD PSALM 48 CALLED "Psalm 23 for city dwellers." At the very least, it contains an incredible invitation to the urban person. It is an invitation to walk. We are invited to walk around the city of God and look. The object of our attention is not the sky or mountains or trees. The object of our attention is the architecture of the city. Not only are we to walk and to look very closely at the buildings, but by filling our eyes with these structures, we can give a testimony to God's existence, His presence in the city, and His care. Wow.

I grew up in Oklahoma. I delight in walking out in an open field, looking off into the distance for miles, and seeing the big sky. Yet I delight in walking down an avenue in Manhattan, seeing the unending rows of windows, and the soaring towers above me. The Bible hints that either experience can be an evidence of God's presence.

Manhattan is a vast, careening complex of almost limitless stories. If I've read a book about subways, all I think of are the subways beneath my feet. With a little turn of mind, all I see are the street trees and the planning that went into putting them where they are supposed to be. Sometimes I look up, and I'm aware of the care and thought put into the gargoyles on the tops of the tenement buildings. At other times I listen to the birds and think about the absurd way the starlings became part of the city landscape. There are mornings when I just look at faces and see misery, fury, and euphoria walk the sidewalks. Artists and advertisers, bankers and shopkeepers, contractors and panhandlers have all jostled and made their stamp on the city. Each one sees something different as he looks around at the same environment.

Streetlights, sidewalk grates, stoplights, stoops, gutters, brickwork. Overlay after overlay, the grids pile up on each other, in an incomprehensible complexity as I walk down one city block. I experience joy and wonder similar to that of hiking in a grand forest. I am refreshed. Not only do I go through the city. The city goes through me.

Can you love the architecture of the city the way you love trees and lakes and open fields? Even the most aesthetically minded New Yorkers, who perhaps objected to the design of many of the skyscrapers, have felt a pang of care in the past for these solid, clumsy giants—the Empire State Building, the Chrysler Building, the Twin Towers. Somehow, these places had become a part of us, and we hadn't even realized it.

When our church took possession of an old building in our area, I remember watching some of the church members using bricks and mortar to seal up some gaping holes in the structure. I remember watching one older lady as she put the bricks into the wet mortar. There is something so deeply satisfying for humans in building. Her expression was both purposeful and content. We are made to love building, to love putting things together piece by piece. It is our nature.

At one point in our work here, some people donated a number of sewing machines. We had a series of sewing workshops in our storefront. Most of the people who came lived in abandoned buildings.

Annie stayed in the corner at first. She wore about six layers of clothing because it was winter and she lived in a squat, an abandoned building that people had taken over illegally from the city. When Annie took off two stocking caps, her hair was frazzled with bits of paper in it as if she slept on garbage. I also learned that where she lived there were no bathroom facilities—only a bucket.

"I don't know why I'm here," she said. "I know I need to do something." Her eyes wandered about the room with a look of fear, like an animal making sure of an escape route. Yet she was by no means frail. "Nothing has worked out lately," she continued. "My boyfriend left. They're about to kick me out of the squat. I've got to go to court. . . ." Her eyes continued to wander to the other people in the room. She looked as though she would bolt at any minute. Her face was like a broken mirror, reflecting a hundred broken thoughts and purposes.

95

Yet, two hours later, I watched her at a sewing machine. A calm purpose governed her every motion. She was making a dress. What she planned to do with the dress, she never told. There was no hesitation, no fear. Instead of an animal, she was a craftsperson, unconscious of the thousand distractions from the people and machines in the little storefront around her. Her world had become a piece of cloth, the few square feet around her and her sewing machine, and all time and commotion had ceased to be. Her satisfaction in her own work overcame all her brokenness and sorrows.

Not only does purpose come when we are making something, a sense of well-being results when something is completed. At one of the locations we use, we needed a place to baptize people. Our mother church donated a huge baptistry tub for us. A group from South Carolina helped install it for us, and all the appropriate questions were relished as we planned together: Can we fit it through the door? Will it fit on the stage? Will it fall through the floor once it's filled with water? Where will we drain it? Can we use the water heater? The answer to the last question was a negative, so we rigged up a hose from a sink to do the job.

Filling it wasn't a pretty sight, but we were so proud at the mission.

People exclaimed as they walked in, "Look how nice it looks!"

"Look at the railing!"

"Our own baptistry!"

Our water system was improvised for the first few baptisms. One Saturday my coworker called me and gave me two options for the baptism the next day. "You can have warm water that is brownblack and you can't see the bottom after you've filled the tub two inches. Or you can have clear water that is ice cold."

The symbolism of dipping our new Christian into dark muddy water to be made clean was too much for me. "Fill it up with cold water," I said with confidence. "It's June and there's a heat wave going on." A miscalculation.

The next day, when I put one foot in the full, clear baptistry, I could not breathe. I had no waders and despite the warm weather, the water felt as though it had come from a mountain stream in January. The church was leaning forward with joy for our new Christian brother and glowing with pride in our new baptistry. I kept descending, but my legs felt like the roof of my mouth feels when I've eaten ice cream too fast.

I was totally in the baptistry and facing the congregation. I wondered if people could pass out from ice shock. My mouth opened and closed as if I were a fish. I tried to speak, but nothing came out.

Finally, I forced a few words out, and Brent, our new Christian, began to walk down the stairs of the baptistry. Brent had a wonderful story of deliverance from crack and was vocal about what Christ had done. He did not like water.

I warned Brent the water would be cold and I urged him, between gasps, to proceed no matter what. As Brent's toe entered the water, I began to hear a continuous high-pitched sound. Did someone's hearing aid have problems? Was the sound system acting up? The earsplitting sound became louder as Brent put his foot farther into the water. It was Brent. It was as if the cold water were squeezing every bit of air out of his lungs like an air mattress. "Don't stop now, keep coming," I said as I reached out to grab his hand. I didn't tell him that I had totally lost feeling in the lower part of my body. My legs were a pair of ice-cold fish sticks by then. How could Brent keep squealing without taking a breath?

The congregation understood what was happening by then and started encouraging Brent. "Don't give up now, Brent. You can do it. You're almost there!"

"Eeeeeeeeeeeeeeeee!" Brent's high-pitched tone got louder as he got deeper in the water, and the sound began to hurt my ears. As soon as his feet hit the bottom of the ice bath, I began to speak really fast. I couldn't help myself. I wondered what the signs for hypothermia were.

People were shouting and clapping. "Don't chicken out! You've almost done it!" As Brent came up after going under the water, his face was as dazed as if he had just been rescued from the

Arctic Sea. Everyone clapped and shouted. Brent's very baptism reenacted the bravery of following Christ.

It didn't matter that the baptistry was second-hand and the water heater didn't work. This baptistry had been installed especially for us. Care was put in its fittings and we loved it. We had a part in designing its installation. Everything about it seemed good to us.

After experiencing such pride in a baptistry, something dawned on me. When we read the Bible, God is always creating. Creation was never meant to be the doctrine of what God did, but what He does. We enjoy the fruits of our labor just as God does. The Bible has a clear and coherent frame. At the beginning, God created light, time, and space (Gen. 1:3–6) and then the world. At the end of the Bible, God is creating a new heaven and a new earth and, of course, a new city (Rev. 21:1–6).

I've heard of a Jewish tradition that there are only three miracles. One miracle is creation. The other miracle is the Last Judgment. The third miracle is everything that happens in between. We're in the in-between time, and God is telling us that He is working a new creation in us (2 Cor. 5:17). I like to think that God is enjoying the process.

God loves to put things together. He's given us the gift of building. Building is a verb and a noun. When we build, our chaotic hearts become focused, intentional, just as Annie's did. When the job is done, we look back with great satisfaction and joy. God made us that way. When we walk in the city, we see the fruits of that work. Even the skyscrapers can sing the glory of God.

CHAPTER 16

The Mending of Creation

You will rebuild those houses
left in ruins for years;
you will be known
as a builder and repairer
of city walls and streets.

ISAIAH 58:12 CEV

God's agenda is the mending of the creation.

KRISTER STENDHAL

PAUL WAS IN PRISON, YET IT SEEMED as though he could hardly contain himself. Even in his grammar in the first of his letter to the church in Ephesus, he was extravagant. With participial phrase piled on participial phrase, relative clause heaped on relative clause, Paul's praise was unstoppable. In Ephesians 1:18, Paul prayed for us, that the eyes of our hearts would be enlightened.

Before that prayer, however, Paul shared the mystery of God's will, God's purpose, God's open secret, God's plan: "to bring all things in heaven and on earth together under one head, even Christ" (Eph. 1:10 NIV). The Amplified Version expands on the meaning of Paul's words: "to unify all things and head them up and consummate them in Christ, both things in heaven and things on earth."

Mending. To bring things together. That's God's agenda. He's doing it though Christ. As Jesus walked the streets, it seemed as though He could hardly restrain himself from mending. A woman touched the hem of His clothing and was healed. A blind man shouts out Jesus' name and can see. Jesus ruined every funeral He went to. As the late preacher and scholar Clarence Jordan once said, "Jesus never made anyone weird." He never added a third leg to a man who was lame or gave a blind man an eye on his forehead. Jesus always brought people to wholeness. And as their bodies mended, their insides mended too. To repair something torn or broken, to restore to good condition, to make whole, to fix—the Bible says this is God's purpose through Christ. Even one of the root meanings for the Hebrew word for *heal* means to "sew together" or "to stitch up." Annie with her sewing machine would have liked that definition.

Ephesians says that God plans to bring together all things through Christ. All things means more than just people. My imagination gets carried away—streets, buildings, trees, planets, galaxies, universes.

When I arrived in the Lower East Side, practically every street had abandoned buildings on them. We worked with squatters, people who had illegally occupied city-owned buildings. The old tenement buildings were in such disrepair that some streets looked as though they had been bombed. Roofs were caved in, cinder blocks covered the doors, windows were broken.

Squatters were trying to find a way to survive the winter. There was no heating system in these old abandoned buildings, and usually no electricity. I am clearly not a construction person. On the roofing crew I worked on as a teenager, everyone had a nickname: *el macho, el gringo, el fuerto*. Mine was the least complementary: *el bendo*, which described my unique abilities with a hammer and a nail. Yet working with these squatters, helping them to find ways to survive in such tough circumstances was strengthening. I felt as though I was a part of God's agenda to mend the city through Christ. Whether we were putting insulation in a wall or fixing a broken window, I thought of Ephesians 1:10.

Through the years in the inner city, Ephesians 1:10 has helped me make it through many rough spots. Whether I was cleaning a toilet, fixing a rat hole, stopping a leak, or picking up after a dog, I have thought, "I am doing my small part in God's plan to bring all things together in Christ here in the city."

Once a church group was helping us clear out a back lot so the kids could play basketball there. It was a very hot, humid summer day; the adjacent brick walls made the little concrete lot feel like an oven. There was a lot of rotten wood and garbage. As the pastor of the church carried a shovel full of garbage, with a dead rat lying on top, he thrust his flushed face close to mine. His cheeks were red and sweaty. "This is hell!" he hissed.

He was right in a way. Yet what he was doing was cleaning up, re-creating out of a hellish place. It was the kind of thing God loves to do, and when we do something like that and see it as a part of God's purpose, an amazing power comes upon us. The Bible says that the gates of hell will not prevail against the church. Jesus assumed we are on the move, invading hell's territory. I like to imagine what happens when we do kick in the gates of hell. We walk in with shovels, start cleaning up, and then start rebuilding.

I have a personal favorite passage in each of the three major prophets in the Old Testament: Ezekiel, Jeremiah, and Isaiah. Each of these passage involves a transformation of the heart. In Ezekiel 36 God promises a heart transplant, removing our hearts of stone: """I will give you a new heart and put a new spirit in you; I will remove from you your heart of stone and give you a heart of flesh. And I will put my Spirit in you and move you to follow my decrees and be careful to keep my laws""" (vv. 26–27 NIV). What a stunning promise to help a rebellious and failing people— hearts that are living and tender again.

In Jeremiah 31, there is a similar promise to work a miracle on the inside, where external pressure from the outside had failed:

"This is the covenant I will make with the house of Israel
    after that time," declares the LORD.
"I will put my law in their minds
    and write it on their hearts.
I will be their God,
    and they will be my people.
No longer will a man teach his neighbor,
    or a man his brother, saying, 'Know the LORD,'
because they will all know me,
    from the least of them to the greatest,"
                declares the LORD.
"For I will forgive their wickedness
    and will remember their sin no more."
(vv. 33–34 NIV)

This is a precious promise to me of what the Lord would do for both the least and the greatest. Everyone will know the Lord. Once more, it emphasizes an inner change, a change of the heart.

Isaiah saw the Suffering Servant wounded for our transgressions in chapter 53. As Isaiah saw the sacrifice of this special one, he came to a life-changing, inward realization about himself and this Redeemer:

We all, like sheep, have gone astray,
    each of us has turned to his own way;
and the LORD has laid on him
    the iniquity of us all. (v. 6 NIV)

All of us, Isaiah realized, have gotten lost by heading in our own directions, and someone else has paid the price. As we see this Suffering One who takes so much unfairly on Himself, an inner acknowledgment and transformation occurs.

For me, these three moments are high points in the ongoing flow of understanding in the Old Testament. Each of these passages is a significant window into what God is doing in the human heart.

Only recently, as I read these three favorite passages of mine, I realized that in the Bible, rebuilding always follows God's work of changing the heart. In the Bible, the rebuilding of cities was especially close to God's heart. In Ezekiel, a few verses after God talked about giving us a new heart, He said: "'On the day that I cleanse you from all your iniquities, I will cause the cities to be inhabited, and the waste places shall be rebuilt'" (Ezek. 36:33 RSV).

As I read this verse a few months ago, my mind's eye could see the abandoned buildings slowly being rebuilt, and spaces where buildings were leveled, slowly being turned into gardens. In the quiet of my study, in a structure that was once an abandoned building itself, I sat and looked at my Bible and realized I had witnessed this very thing happen in my own neighborhood!

Likewise in Jeremiah, after the astonishing passage in which God promised to write His law on the Israelites' hearts so that all would know the Lord, I found this promise: "'The days are coming,' declares the LORD, 'when this city will be rebuilt for me'" (Jer. 31:38 NIV). God also gave specific instructions for that time—"'from the Tower of Hananel to the Corner Gate.'"

At the high point of Jeremiah's understanding of a new covenant, God gave the promise of rebuilding the city. As I sat at my desk, I excitedly looked to see what followed my third favorite passage in the Old Testament, the passage in which Isaiah described so specifically the atoning death of a Special One and our change of heart as we realize He died for our sins. Was there any promise for abandoned neighborhoods?

Sure enough, there it was, just following one of the most famous passages in the Bible:

"Enlarge the place of your tent,
and let the curtains of your habitations be stretched out;
hold not back, lengthen your cords
and strengthen your stakes.
For you will spread abroad to the right and to the left,
and your descendants will possess the nations
and will people the desolate cities." (Isa. 54:2–3 RSV)

Another promise for the desolate cities. What I saw before my eyes was the flow from a changed heart to a concern for the cities, a desire to re-people and rebuild desolate places.

This consistent concern for the rebuilding of the city flows right into the New Testament. When Jesus began His ministry in Nazareth, in the Gospel of Luke, the people in the synagogue gave Him the book of the prophet Isaiah. Luke tells us that Jesus found the place where Isaiah talked about the Spirit working to tell good news to the poor, proclaim release to the captives, recovery of sight to the blind, and liberty to the oppressed (Luke 4:17–19). What an explosive, powerful passage. As I read Isaiah 61:1–2, which Jesus quoted, I continued to read the next verse. Verse 3 talks about how this work of the Spirit will change the heart, will give flowers instead of sorrow, joyous praise in place of broken hearts. How does one of Jesus' favorite passages close?

After the change of heart, sure enough, there it is again in verse 4: These changed people

will rebuild the ancient ruins
and restore the places long devastated;
they will renew the ruined cities
that have been devastated for generations. (NIV)

As I read these verses, I sense more closely the personality of God, His great urge to mend hearts and cities. The empty, partially abandoned buildings of the Lower East Side were the visible manifestations of the burned-out, hollow lives of many of the people who lived here. God is not done yet. The source for this rebuilding is still the same. "By a carpenter mankind was made, and only by that carpenter can mankind be remade."[17]

When I came to New York, I had a supervisor who was a father figure to me. Ray looked out for me. He showed me the ropes both in Harlem and the Lower East Side. I can remember walking with him down the streets, my eyes as big as frying pans, taking in the shouts, the arguments from upper windows, the shopkeepers guarding their fruit, the beggars, and the police. Ray always walked with purpose and commitment. But Ray had one embarrassing habit.

If there was a big pile of garbage, sometimes Ray would stop and examine it. Then, as people rushed past him, he would take a small step in for a closer look. The noise of the street seemed far away from him then. Eventually, like someone reaching into an aquarium to grab a fish, he would reach into the sea of junk and pull a stick of furniture or piece of wood out. Sometimes it was a broken chair or a part of a table. Then without hesitation, he would tuck his treasure under his arm and proceed to walk with his customary purpose and focus.

I would tease Ray about this habit. "Ray, you are a garbage man! Every trash heap is a grab bag for you!" I would say. "Don't they pay you enough salary? You're embarrassing me. I'm going to pretend like I don't know you the next time I see you going through someone's trash."

Ray would just laugh and keep walking. Later I visited Ray's home. It was beautiful. Ray took me to his workroom. There was a row of broken furniture, projects Ray was working on. He showed me how he was replacing a leg of an old chair and regluing all the pieces of the chair so that everything fit snugly. He showed me how he was taking about six layers of paint off another chair, so I could see the beautiful wood grain beneath the crust. His eyes sparkled and his manner warmed as he talked about how long it took to recane a bench or craft a replacement part.

As we returned to his living room, I looked around again. The chairs, the tables, the cabinets all had a golden glow. "Every single piece of furniture here," Ray said, "is made of solid oak. And every single piece came from the trash piles of New York City."

Now I've been converted. I go through the garbage too. I've learned that God loves to mend, and God is the greatest ragpicker in the universe, because He takes broken people like you and me and makes something beautiful out of us.

Living in the city helped me to read the Bible more deeply and learn more about God's essential love for building and rebuilding. I began to see God's work of re-creating not only in people, but in everything. A new sense of vision settled in my heart as I saw a little more clearly how our small acts fit together in God's purposeful love. But none of that really prepared me for the next phase in my life in Manhattan.

CHAPTER 17

The Dust of Death

You lay me in the dust of death.

PSALM 22:15B NIV

When Dante is in Heaven, he looks down and sees the tiny earth, the "threshing floor that makes us so fierce."

CANTO 22, THE DIVINE COMEDY: PARADISE

THE THREE-DAY TRAUMATOLOGY CLASS at Columbia University began to drag. It was about six months after the World Trade Center tragedy, and our staff was continuing to try to get as much training as possible. Someone had called me a few days earlier and said, "You know, I have a big map of Manhattan here, and I've been doing some measuring. Do you know that your mission is exactly five thousand feet from Ground Zero?" I thanked him for the information.

The traumatology class was eight hours a day. The speaker had worked with many victims from the Oklahoma City bombing. The discussion of disaster and recovery from disaster made me think about September 11 over and over again. Sure enough, as the speaker talked about how a disaster will trigger sorrow from other grief in a person's life, I became sadder and sadder.

I began to think about people who had died in the past few years. I thought about the death of my mom. I sat at the conference table and felt waves of sadness for people who had given their lives on September 11. I looked around the room and saw that I wasn't alone.

In the months preceding the conference, I was surprised by the anger I felt. I was angry because my older son went to school a couple of blocks away from the World Trade Center. He had watched five people die at close range on that day. These people had died, not from a tragic accident, but out of intentional malice. I was angry that my son, who, after a few weeks, continued to go to school close to Ground Zero, had respiratory problems for months after the tragedy, with the typical "World Trade Center cough." I remember standing outside my son's school, six weeks after the tragedy, smelling that terrible smell of burned Sheetrock, clenching my teeth in choked fury, which I couldn't really articulate.

I was angry because the children we work with in our mission acted out so much more after September 11. Since we were in the lockdown area for the first few days, cars and nonresidents couldn't come to our neighborhoods. Children, picking up the fears of their caregivers, were afraid another building would explode and that there wouldn't be enough food at the grocery stores again.

After September, every child in every one of our tutoring sites said his biggest fear was that he would either burn to death or his building would explode. Fears were very active with the children. For example, when our tutors were taking one child home, the elevator stopped momentarily between floors. The child screamed in a high-pitched shriek, "Let me out! Let me out!" Some children, who had a great deal of family turmoil, seemed to go over the edge. One eight-year-old child wrote a suicide note.

All the stories I had heard as a pastor in Lower Manhattan following the tragedy had a cumulative effect as I sat in the classroom. People who had lost a brother, niece, or husband, others who had been in the towers on September 11, others who had worked close by and found they couldn't function normally afterward—all of these stories crowded in on me as I sat trying to take notes.

"It is important to help move the images from the right-brain, intuitive side of your thinking to the left-brain, language side," the teacher explained. Sure enough, as he spoke, I began to see images I had forgotten, images as I walked inside the smoke near Ground Zero after the second tower collapsed, trying to make sure my son was OK.

On the morning of September 11, I was in my office when my wife Susan called. "Turn on the TV," she said. "The World Trade Center is burning." She was walking to work and could see it happening. At each corner of her walk to the subway, people were crowding around in order to see better. She eventually saw what appeared to be tiny furniture falling from the towers. She looked closer and saw that the falling objects were people.

I turned on the TV and ran outside to look. From our corner, I could see the smoke billowing from the tower. As I went back upstairs, I heard the boom as the second plane hit.

It was only then that I really began to worry about my older son Freeman, who went to school only a couple of blocks away from the towers. Susan called again, and I decided to run to our apartment a few blocks away, because that was probably the first place Freeman would call. As I trotted home, people were standing together at any place where they could see the towers through the other buildings. No one was talking; no one was laughing. They were as mute as statues.

When I got home, I was told by a coworker that the radio had said the school was letting students out only if their parents came to pick them up. I desperately checked through my options. I had no car. I couldn't take a taxi. Taxis couldn't go down there. All the subways and buses were shut down in that area. Walking was way too slow for me to endure.

I thought of my younger son's bike. I took it from its place, hanging from the ceiling. I stopped to watch a replay of the collapse of the first tower on TV. The urge in my chest to make sure my son was OK became almost unbearable.

The second tower must have collapsed when I was bringing the bike through the hallway. I jumped on the bike and pedaled like a maniac toward the towers. I wondered why I couldn't see the other tower. Those looming structures were what usually guided me to Freeman's school. I soon discovered that the brakes didn't work on my son's bike, but that thought couldn't stop me. As I pedaled down the avenues toward the mountain of smoke, I looked into the faces of thousands of people heading north, walking away from Ground Zero.

They looked like war refugees. No one was talking. The faces looked stunned, weary, and protective. As I headed farther south toward the smoke, I saw more and more people sprinkled in the crowd who were covered with white dust or debris. Even though the walkers weren't talking, there was a lot of noise—sirens, police directing traffic, people shouting instructions.

I came to a checkpoint. Roadblocks were up and police were doing their job. "My son's at Stuyvesant High School!" I pleaded. They let me through. I turned corners, switched streets, avoiding major barricades of official vehicles. The mountain of smoke seemed huge now. I was stopped by a number of other police as I got closer and closer to Ground Zero, but they all mercifully let me pass to try to find my son.

Strangely enough, at that point in time, the closer I got to Ground Zero, the quieter things became. No one stopped me now; just a few emergency workers ran across the intersections. By this time I was only two blocks away from Freeman's school and about a block away from Ground Zero. I was in a smoky haze, and the huge, massive wall of smoke that towered above me was very close. Everything was deathly quiet. The only other times I had remembered New York being quiet like that was after a blanket of fresh, new-fallen snow covered the ground.

Where I was, an inch of fine powder covered sidewalks, the streets, everything. It was not until later that I realized that the powder was absorbing the sound, just like snow. Just as snow can make a familiar street look wonderfully different, so this white powder made a well-known corner look horribly changed.

Everything was quiet and time seemed frozen. Two rescue workers ran across my path, but they weren't looking at me. I searched for a way to get to Freeman's high school without going into that wall of debris and smoke. I did not want to go into that smoke. I did not want to be in a place where I could not see where I was stepping. Also, the workers had masks on, and I remember thinking, *What am I inhaling?* But I had not come that far to stop.

I got off the bike and covered my face with my shirt. I walked into the smoky debris. I was all alone and it was still quiet. It seemed I was in the debris for an eternity. I could hardly see or breathe. I felt my way for about a block. These were the memories I had forgotten for about six months. It was a silent, ghostly, deadly experience. Before I got to the school, I came out of the smoke. I could see and breathe better. There was a lot of noise and activity around the school; police and emergency workers were running in and out. "Are the students OK?" I clutched a policeman's arm. "Everyone was evacuated safely," he said. I asked four other people the same question, just to make sure.

I felt a wave of relief. The principal was arguing with authorities in the back of the school. I still had to find my son, but in order to do so, I needed to head away from the epicenter of the trauma. As I walked away, I saw a firefighter with a water hose. He was spraying a coworker. "Hose yourself down!" he shouted to others. "You don't know what was in that s——." I realized that I, too, was now covered with debris.

I rode the bike to where the authorities said they had taken the students. No one there knew anything about them. After waiting a long time, I went home and waited for Freeman to call.

I remembered the firefighter's instructions, and I stepped into the shower with all my clothes on. I longed to wash all the events of the morning off too. I wiped the white dust off my shoes. *The dust of death*, I thought numbly.

My son finally called. He had to wait in line at a pay phone for a long time. "Is it OK if I bring my friends with me?" he asked. "They have nowhere to go."

"How many are there?" I asked.

"About fourteen."

Fourteen football players crammed themselves into the living room of our tiny apartment. Freeman's story stunned me. At close range, from the window of his classroom, he watched three people fall to their deaths. He saw two people waving white clothing, trying to catch someone's attention. He watched the black smoke engulf them, and they were gone. As the students at his school evacuated, the second tower collapsed. The wall of smoke and debris rushed toward the students, and they broke into a run. They did outrun it and found themselves in Lower Manhattan, left to their own devices in order to get home. His teammates had waited for each other, and he brought them home with him. The students crammed close together on the floor of our living room, watched the news, and talked and talked.

As I walked to get pizza for the teenagers, a verse from Scripture kept coming to mind: "Men's anger only results in more praise for you" (Ps. 76:10 TEV). Some scholars think that the verse means God is so great that He can bring good out of even the worst things. "What is meant to terrorize us will make us braver. What is meant to divide us will unite us. What is meant to humiliate us will bring us closer to God," I said to myself. All the shops and food places on First Avenue were pitching in to make things easier for the thousands on foot, stuck in Manhattan. No one was gouging people; everyone was working together. Even the pizzas were handed over in record time, and the lines were friendly.

Eventually all the students got home, some having to walk for hours. My wife had her own saga, struggling to find a way to get to the Bronx to pick up my younger son Owen. She found a taxi, which got her to the bridge, but it was blocked. Then she walked across the bridge and amazingly found another taxi. Owen and Susan had to reverse the process to get home. It took many hours. By the end of the day, we were all back in Lower Manhattan in our precious home.

Our area was in a lockdown. No cars or nonresidents could come here. The next day, we put food and a TV outside our mission as people walked the streets. Inside was a prayer room. People just wanted to talk.

"I go down there every day," one man said. "As I left, a man not far from me was hit by a flying chair, of all things. Killed him right away. Why did I walk away safe, and now he's dead?"

Another man told me that first day, "I was cleaning up an office. All my friends went down the exit, but I went across the office to call my wife. After I called her, I went down the other exit. I lived, but all my friends are missing. I've got to do something."

The stories kept coming thick and fast. In the stream of people during the next few days, one woman stands out vividly in my mind. She was completely covered with tattoos. Every inch of skin was marked with images of color. She had a look of deep anxiety, as she stood in the middle of a crowd of people. "I run a tattoo shop," she said. "But now everything I do seems so, so . . . superficial." She looked straight at me with deep earnestness. I had hardly said anything. "I know I need the Lord." As we talked and eventually prayed to ask Christ into her life, a thought kept coming to me. Even though this woman and I were incredibly *un*like each other in occupation, in outlook, and in friends, in one way we were just alike. We both, in one way or another, had a tendency to find meaning and purpose in things that are, in the end, superficial. They are only skin-deep. Whether our goals are a career, tattoos, art, or reputation, none of these things are able to bear the burden of our hearts as we look into the eyes of tragedy.

The gut-grabbing urge not to allow this tragedy to have its intended effect surprised me too. A little over a week after September 11, I was scheduled to perform a wedding for a couple who were very dear to me. In those early days after the occurrence, the extended families had legitimate concerns about coming into Manhattan for the wedding.

"What should we do?" the bride-to-be asked. "Should we move the wedding to some safer place or postpone it?" The couple decided to have the wedding in Manhattan on schedule.

The wedding went off without a hitch. The moment that I remember best, however, was when the bride and groom walked down the stairs outside the church. All the cars passing by began to honk. People stuck their heads out windows and shouted as if they had just seen the game-winning touchdown at the Super Bowl. Even though the smell of the burning towers still cloaked the area, people hoarsely bellowed, "Way to go! Don't let them stop you! That's the spirit!" The traffic stop became a victory parade. I had never seen anything like it in the city. But something made me want to roll up my sleeves and celebrate this occasion of love and hope as if our lives depended on it. And maybe lives did depend on it.

I knew people needed to talk about the tragedy. But I had heard so many stories of fear, of heartache, of wondering. I would tell people, "Any experience can either drive us away from God or draw us closer to God. Let's allow this horrible thing to draw us closer to God." Yet the stories of others took a deeper toll on me than I realized. Sometimes, after a long day, I felt like a garbage truck that had more and more debris compacted into it. I wasn't really dumping garbage. There was just more and more sorrow pushed into me. I remember after Christmas, just sitting in a chair and staring off into space. I felt immobilized.

Everyone in the city was more aware of the fragility of our situation. Some of our friends left for a while. The granite buildings and solid towers I loved so much seemed far less permanent after September. But the awareness of the fragility of the city is nothing new. I reread a famous essay on New York City, written by E. B. White in the summer of 1948. After September 11, the words he chose in his closing passage seemed eerily familiar:

> The subtlest change in New York is something people don't speak much about but that is in everyone's mind. The city, for the first time in its long history, is destructible. A single flight of planes no bigger than a wedge of geese can quickly end this island fantasy, burn the towers, crumble the bridges, turn the underground passages into lethal chambers, cremate the millions. The intimation of mortality is part of New York now: in the sound of the jets overhead, in the black headlines of the latest edition.

> All dwellers in cities must live with the stubborn fact of annihilation; in New York the fact is somewhat more concentrated because of the concentration of the city itself, and because, of all targets, New York has a certain clear priority. In the mind of whatever perverted dreamer might loose the lightning, New York must hold a steady, irresistible charm.[18]

In closing, White reflected on the irony of the fact that New York City is the place where people also try to talk out the problems of the world, such as at the United Nations. It is the current, heartbreaking paradox of the city:

The city at last perfectly illustrates both the universal dilemma and the general solution, this riddle
in steel and stone is at once the perfect target and
perfect demonstration of nonviolence, of racial
brotherhood, this lofty target scraping the skies and
meeting the destroying planes halfway, home of all
people and all nations, capital of everything, housing
the deliberations by which the planes are to be
stayed and their errand forestalled.[19]

In this sense, everything has not changed since September 11.
The foreboding of the fragility of the city has been there before.
What was new for me was the sense of anger, rage, sadness, and
confusion that roared around inside me like a hurricane.

I found help for my thoughts from a rabbi. He is dead now,
but his words continue to strike home. I was thumbing through a
small anthology of the writings of Abraham Joshua Heschel. He
was born in Warsaw, Poland, and eventually escaped to America in
1939. The introduction mentioned that he had lost his family and
community in the fires of World War II. The loss, the bloodshed he
experienced, seemed almost unspeakable, and yet he spoke.

It looked as though the book was published in 1954. He had
years to come to terms with his own loss and with the loss of those
around him. As I thumbed through the excerpt, Heschel asked the
question concerning the evil he experienced: "Who is responsible?"

His answer touched me by its humility. He quoted another
rabbi who said, "If a man has beheld evil, he may know that it was
shown to him in order that he learn his own guilt and repent; for
what is shown to him is also within him."[20]

The words continued to leap out at me with a strange rele-
vance. He talked about our failure to speak in the times long preceding the Holocaust. "Where were we," he asked, "when raving
madmen were sowing wrath in the hearts of the unemployed?"

I considered those words as I sat in the conference room at
Columbia and thought about Heschel. Wrath. "I just can't accept

that someone is so angry at me," a stunned undergraduate who lives in Manhattan told the leader and the group. Wrath.

The next words Heschel said about his own experience continued to ring in my ears for months: "We have failed to fight *for* right, *for* justice, *for* goodness; as a result we must fight *against* wrong, *against* injustice, *against* evil."[21] These words made sense to me in my own situation. I knew in my heart that if we did not fight for what was right for the children I saw on the streets in New York, we would end up fighting against them as grown-up drug dealers and perpetrators of violent crime. In problems concerning the city, I always thought it was more important to put a fence at the top of the cliff rather than going to the expense of building a hospital (and a prison!) at the bottom of the cliff.

In Manhattan, as well as across the country, there was a swirling desire to do something. I would receive phone calls in the months following, with people asking, "What can we do?" I began to carry with me through the day a shortened version of Heschel's comment: If I do not fight *for* what is right, I end up fighting *against* what is wrong. The experience in Lower Manhattan was close enough to me that sometimes I could not watch the images of the tragedy on TV. But I learned this from a rabbi's loss in World War II. He said, "A good person is not he who does the right thing, but he who is in the habit of doing the right thing."[22] In some small way, each of us can be as brave as a firefighter, a policeman, or a soldier overseas. We have the opportunity, each day to live sacrificially in developing the habit of fighting for what is right.

I listened to one preacher speak about the seemingly intractable and unsolvable problems concerning wrath in our world, and especially in our cities today. He said that we all know that in order to fight malaria, the best solution is not to kill mosquitoes. The best solution is to drain the swamp. No doubt we must do everything possible to fight against the immediate destructive power of the disease. We just can't forget to think about draining the swamp.

All these thoughts came to the surface as I was forced to sit still in the classroom at Columbia and think about disasters. The face of one of the persons in our church came into sharp focus. He lived in our neighborhood, and he told the story of fleeing to Vermont after September 11. "The image of the explosion stayed in my mind," he said. "It was not the explosion itself that bothered me, I simply felt that the steel girders inside of *me* were melting every time I saw it." Then he told his agonizing journey of spiritual renewal in Vermont and his return to Lower Manhattan. He looked me straight in the face. "The World Trade Center tragedy brought me so much closer to God."

As I walked along my own street returning from my final day of traumatology training at Columbia, I looked down the block. There were little American flags hanging from some of the windows, but after six months of winter weather, they looked faded and tattered. There were decals of flags on many of the other windows, but they had begun to peel. The national surge of emotion following the tragedy had also begun to fade. The world seems gripped in a vise of anger, and no one knows what the coming years will bring. Yet the Lord has used even this horrible tragedy to help change the way I see the city and the way I live each day. It helped me develop a new habit—looking for ways in each moment to fight *for* what is right in the place where I am, in order to keep us all from fighting in the future *against* so much that is wrong.

CHAPTER 18

Stopping to Start

The promise to enter the place of rest is still good, and we must take care that none of you miss out.

HEBREWS 4:1 CEV

The object of life is not to side with the majority, but to escape from finding yourself in the ranks of the insane.

MARCUS AURELIUS

119

THE HEARTACHE SURROUNDING the World Trade Center will continue to take its toll for years and for lifetimes. It is taking its toll on me. "If you don't carve out time for rest, no one else will," blind Marty told me on the street in his very unsubtle manner. The experiences of the last years have led my family and my church more deeply into God's rhythm of activity and rest.

It was an August night in the city. The muggy smog seemed to encase me in steam. I had worked too long, and now I was rushing off and sweating to do something else. The herd of bodies bounced off each other on the sidewalk. Several layers of bodies ahead, I saw the name, Lombardi on the back of a yellow T-shirt. I craned my soggy neck to see the full name—V. Lombardi. This is what I needed, an inspiring quote from one of the master motivators.

I shoved my way through slick masses of flesh to see the quote: "Fatigue"—someone got in the way—"makes cowards of us all." That was it. That was for me. It was graffiti on a moving wall. I had been trying to do too much.

In our Bible studies in the inner city, people have often talked about the acronym HALT, which many learned from their Alcoholics Anonymous meetings. If you're hungry, angry, lonely, or tired, then it is time to stop. You are very vulnerable in your area of difficulty, regardless of what that area is.

I have learned in the city that when I am tired, I become easily angry or fearful or contemptuous. It's as if my brakes lock, and every problem seems intractable. On that night, the cake I was supposed to pick up was not ready. The store where I was to buy a gift was closed. The air conditioner was broken in the card store and my shirt became soaked with perspiration. I was late. Every circumstance seemed to fan the flame of my anger at the universe. Every problem drove me deeper into a conviction that there were no solutions and never would be.

These feelings, for me, are the result of fatigue. It was time for me to halt. I needed to stop in order to start. I continue to be amazed to see what a night's sleep, or an hour of rest, can do for my perspective. Rest helps us see things differently. When my wife and I were two-year missionaries in Hong Kong, we sometimes heard our friends say something like this: "Muddy waters, when still, become clear." The Bible says this in a thousand ways—"It is in vain that you rise up early and go late to rest, / eating the bread of anxious toil; / for he gives to his beloved sleep" (Ps. 127:2 RSV).

My wife works at a university with a number of rabbis. They began to tell her what the Sabbath meant to them. On the day of rest, they explained, they cannot perform any actions that produce things. They cannot write a letter, turn on a light, or cook. They can't ride in a car or talk on the phone. They can take a walk with their families or throw the football around or make love with their spouse or take a nap. The Sabbath rules always seemed oppressive and binding when I heard about them in Sunday school as a child.

From my new perspective, as an exhausted, frenzied, city-fried adult, the boundaries for rest seemed lovely, precious. Behind our apartment is a synagogue. One time I slipped into the Friday night service. The Sabbath for those celebrants began at sundown on Friday. The people were friendly and joyous. They seemed so excited that they were about to have a day of rest. I felt again the excitement of a child being let out of school on Friday. Saturday stretched before me like an eternity of fun and release from drudgery. There was a lot of Hebrew in the service, but I remember the people saying something like this: "Come, Queen Sabbath."

The day of rest is royal. It is a queen. It is a time to halt, to stop. How practical. What wonderful boundaries to keep us from feeling as though we have to make that one last phone call, type that one last E-mail, write that one last letter, pay that one last bill. How gracious of our Lord, how tender, to make a day of rest one of the Ten Commandments.

"I can't talk to you on the phone on my day off for the next month," I told my brother. "I'm following what I understand of the Hasidic rules for the Sabbath for four weeks."

These comments were a release for my brother. He was released from any doubt that I was a totally bizarre fanatic, teetering on the edge of sanity.

For the next four weeks, my wife and I took walks on our rest day, as well as naps. We had time to talk. We ate simply, things that didn't need to be cooked. We read and prayed. We even, for one brief period each week, adjusted ourselves back to the normal rhythm of day and night, refusing to turn on and off the electric lights. We talked about what we had done in the week and stamped value on the things that were good.

It was healing. Although we are by no means Hasidic, we still continue to put boundaries on one day a week when we were not frantically working to fulfill our thousands of petty commitments. As we did this, I began to remember things. I remembered something my mother told me as a child. My mother was born in China. My grandfather was a medical missionary there. My mom could speak Chinese more easily than English when she was young. She used to employ a phrase she said she could not translate into English. The phrase from her dialect was *wong wong*. It did not exactly mean "rest." It was the opposite of goofing off. According to my mom, it meant something more like "the art of leisure." It was the art of resting after having worked hard. It was the wise ability to really enjoy yourself without having to work. To *wong wong* was not to do some routine drudgery; it was a mature sense of grace and pleasure in time not wracked by what we should be doing. That is, at least, what I remember from what she said. Now as an adult, I wanted to learn more about how to *wong wong*.

I understand now, better, why we need the tender commandment[23] for a day of rest. When the urban activities and projects reach a frantic pitch, my wife will say, "Remember they stoned people in the Old Testament when they didn't take a day of rest." Perhaps it was not the message of gentle grace I wanted to hear, but she got her point across. I started to learn to rest by simply resting.

In contrast to God's thoughtful guidelines, the city tempts us never to rest. As I walked along an avenue of the city, the active hum of cars, construction, radios, and conversation could often make my heart sing. I, too, became part of this song of the city, as I watched things being done that ten or a hundred or a thousand humans could not do. In this stew of thousands of people bubbling with movement, something happened that went beyond the solitary worker.

Yet this activity had its dark side. In the city that never sleeps, this activity can become pathological. Marcus Aurelius pointed out the thrust of our lives can't be simply to do what everyone else is doing around us. In fact, it may be that what the majority of people are doing is really a kind of insanity. To be caught up in the mad rush of the city may be idiocy.

Thinking about the collective energy in the city made me turn again to people outside the city who had lost their way. As I read stories about finding people who got lost in the woods, I learned something I already knew in my heart. Often, when people discover they are lost in a forest, they tend to move faster and faster. Rather than stopping in one place and sensibly waiting for help, they sometimes run in a frenzy. This becomes a dangerous time as lost people become more weary and frantic. Sometimes injuries occur. One tracker described how sometimes when lost people are found, they will continue to run from the person sent to rescue them. They have worked themselves into such a state that they will even run from family members. Somehow, it is part of our nature, that when we get lost, we quicken our pace. The people I watched on the street in my city began to look like lost people running faster and faster.

The chaplains and psychologists I have talked to since September 11 informed me that whatever part of us we deny in life will return, knife in hand, demanding a sacrifice. If you never take a time to rest, then sickness will rise up and become your rest. If you deny the warnings of your experience for a long, long time, then death rises up and becomes the final pause on earth. I thought about grief and sorrow and began to understand that some people in the city never stopped running.

I had known Vera for a long time. "How you doing, Pastor? How's your family? You're looking good. Everything OK at the church? Thanks for praying for my family." Her talk was always one long stream of encouragement. Never did I hear her ever say any-thing discouraging or depressing, but sometimes she talked too fast, as if she were on the run.

She was always on the run, from her family, from addiction, from her personal demons, and finally from disease. She had been in and out of hospitals and programs more times than she could count. She never seemed to rest, nor could she. Calamity and sick-ness had become her rest.

She was in the hospital again, and I went by to see her. "Oh, Pastor," she said, "I was just sleeping, but I have been wanting to talk to you so much. Did you know I was in a coma for four days? It was really bad. They thought I was going to die. That whole time I was dreaming, and this is what I dreamed—I was going through a long dark tunnel. It was terrible. Finally I got to the end of the tun-nel, and I poked my head out. I was in the city, but it was awful. It was a dark slum with gangs roaming about and vicious dogs and children crying and people trying to hurt each other. It was so real and I wanted to get out of there so bad. I knew what it was. It was hell. I had died and gone to hell. It was all the worst things about the city. I felt like I stayed there for the longest time. Finally I came out of the coma. I was so glad." Her eyes got wider as she told the story. "I prayed that you would come. This is no joke. I don't ever want there to be any possibility that I would go to that place again. I think this was a warning. I want to be sure that Christ is in my life. No more pretending. No word games. Would you pray with me right now?"

We prayed, and Vera gave me permission to tell her story. I wish I could say that everything went perfectly for Vera after that, but she had some ups and downs. For a brief time, she was on the street again. She had been very, very sick. Finally she died.

The funeral service was in a small funeral home in the area. Everyone pitched in because there wasn't a lot of money. The place was packed, however, by people who wanted to remember Vera's encouragement, laughter, and sense of humor. We knew she was not running anymore. An old pastor came from the church in the neighborhood where she grew up. He looked as though he had seen many, many untimely deaths from drugs, AIDS, and violence. He seemed accustomed to seeing that each person's life is filled with both marvelous things and very horrible things.

"I've been a pastor a long time," he shared. "What I know is precious little, but it is very precious. This is what I have learned." He paused for a moment and everyone was quiet. "Death is not a period, it's a comma. What we think is the end is not really the end, and it's not the end for Vera." In its own way, the funeral became a celebration of how God's mercy worked in very wretched circumstances.

That funeral home, somehow, had become a moment of rest and regrouping for every person there, even though the traffic and pedestrians rushed by outside through the whole service. The fatigue of working could keep us from thinking, but not forever. Because of Vera's death, each of us was forced to stop and reflect about the deepest things of life. Looking into Vera's face in the coffin, remembering her funny jokes, thinking about what she was running from—it all made me ask again the ultimate question. Is this death we see an end point or a passageway? Is it a stop or a pause? A period or a comma? Were the deaths at the World Trade Center a few blocks away from here the final note of a sad song or a prelude? If we never stop, we never have to think about these questions.

I sat there in that old funeral home and thought of how Vera was always on the run. In that room there was a pause, but it was not the end. Only God knows what the final phase will bring for Vera. I sat and thought of all the people on the run on the streets outside, each looking for God like a thief looks for a policeman, going faster and faster until their light in the city is finally extinguished. That stop is only a comma, however.

After the funeral, I walked out on the street and noticed the people around me racing by, desperate not to be lost. The further away from peace we get, the more exhausted we become. The instruction in the Bible for taking rest seems different to me now. Instead of looking oppressive, the instructions seem sane.

In the following days, I began to look for places where people could stop. Few places in the city are at the service of quiet and rest. Sometimes cathedrals and churches are there for quiet. Sometimes art museums work hard to be an empty space where you can stand, be quiet, and look. Sometimes a park with trees can be a place of quiet, if it is not filled with the noise of a sports event or the obnoxious blaring of a boom box.

Even though I loved the activity of the city, I began to crave the quiet. Good sense in the Bible provided the answer. All my adult life I had quoted Isaiah 58, but now I finally started to understand it. In this chapter, God tells His people what true religious practices are: "'The kind of fasting I want is this: Remove the chains of oppression and the yoke of injustice, and let the oppressed go free. Share your food with the hungry and open your homes to the homeless poor. Give clothes to those who have nothing to wear, and do not refuse to help your own relatives. . . . If you give food to the hungry and satisfy those who are in need, then the darkness around you will turn to the brightness of noon'" (vv. 6–7, 10 TEV).

Surely there is no doubt in these verses that we are to be doers. The message is not an endless argument about theories. It tells us what we are to be doing, very specifically. Even though I've quoted these verses in thanking people as they reach out to others, I've never really paid attention to how the chapter begins or ends.

After Vera's death, I began to notice that the chapter begins with the delight in worship, however skewed that worship may be. Although God's voice is a bit ironic here, He says,

"Yet day after day they seek me
        and delight to know my ways, . . .
    they delight to draw near to God." (Isa. 58:2 NRSV)

The people worship and do not see because their worship is not connected to service. But as I have watched, year after year, workers helping provide food and clothing for hurting people in the city, my heart has read again about the "delight" in verse 2. I've come to realize that without the delight in worship, all our service eventually becomes merely a process of our handing out our own emptiness. Delighting in God in worship is at the core of our purpose. The other things can only flow out of glorifying God and enjoying God forever.

I heard about a French farmer who had retired and spent time in a small chapel on a hill each day. "What are you doing for so long up there each day?" his friends asked.

"Well," the farmer said, "I look at God, and God looks at me, and we are both happy." Looking at God, and having God look at me became the essence of delight in worship. Without this delight in worship, our service becomes as effective as an arm or leg that has been amputated. Yet the point of the first verses in Isaiah 58 is that worship without service is nothing but a torso. It is only half a body and does not function properly.

Earlier it had become clear to me that in looking out for those who are in difficult situations, we become rebuilders in the truest sense of the word: "Your people will rebuild what has long been in ruins, building again on the old foundations. You will be known as the people who rebuilt the walls, who restored ruined houses" (Isa. 58:12 TEV).

I thought I understood the chapter, a natural flow from worship to service that cannot be divided. In fact, they are all part of the same fabric. But I had not seriously read the end of the chapter:

If you refrain from trampling the sabbath,
      from pursuing your own interests on my holy day;
if you call the sabbath a delight." (Isa. 58:13 NRSV)

There's that word *delight* again. How strange. Part of the strong emphasis on service in this chapter is the encouragement to call rest a delight. I know in my own life, in my anxious frenzy of urban service, I had not called rest a delight. I had been caught up in the city's motion. Like speeding in a go-cart, the faster I went, the less I saw.

The words of this chapter about service had always seemed to me so vibrant, so relevant, so contemporary. But, as I continued to read the chapter, I realized that what once seemed to me an archaic notion, the Sabbath, was what made the other portions relevant. Without a Sabbath, work in the city made no sense; Vera's life made no sense. Even our grief over the deaths at the World Trade Center made little sense, without times of rest.

Isaiah goes on. If I respect a time to stop and rest, then I will take delight in the Lord (Isa. 58:13–14, paraphrased). I am back to the beginning of the chapter again—delighting in the Lord. I look at God and God looks at me. This is the core of worship.

When I was a boy, I heard stories of Paul Bunyan and the Round River, a river that brought him back to where he started. It flowed and flowed in a circle, seeming to find renewal in itself. As I work in the city now, Isaiah 58 has become for me a refreshing circular river. It has shown me the natural and necessary rhythm of worship to service to rest to worship. As we step into this river, in the middle of the city, we see that the different parts of Isaiah 58, like different sections of water in a river, all merge and become the same. It is delightful.

CHAPTER 19

Whistling Jack
Says Thank You

*Do not be anxious about anything, but in everything, by
prayer and petition, with thanksgiving, present your
requests to God.*

PHILIPPIANS 4:6 NIV

*There is a way of ordering our mental life on more than
one level at once. On one level we may be thinking,*

129

> *discussing, seeing, calculating, meeting all the*
> *demands of external affairs. But deep within, behind*
> *the scenes, at a profounder level, we may be in prayer*
> *and adoration, song and worship, and a gentle*
> *receptiveness to divine breathings.*
>
> THOMAS R. KELLY

WHISTLING JACK SAT UNDER the same tree for years in the park. At one time, he had been a surgeon at a hospital in the city, but drinking had changed all that. After years of Jack's homelessness and tragedies, Christ had taken root in his heart. Even though he was an old man, he kept sitting under the tree, and he always loved to talk. He also enjoyed the Bible immensely.

Whistling Jack has been dead for years, but people who knew him still pause to remember him when they walk by the tree. I stop and remember, too, when I walk by. My memories of my conversations with Whistling Jack are now a fusion of what he said, what people said he said, and mostly what I've said myself as my heart learns to see. But, when I walk by that tree, his face and his words all come into focus in my mind's eye.

"This is the key," Whistling Jack said. He adjusted himself as he sat on the huge root of the old black locust tree. His face was as gnarled as the bark on the tree. "The power," he continued, "flows through your thanks, not through your requests." He was placing some handkerchiefs on the grass around him to dry in the sun. He carefully placed each one of them parallel to his socks, which were also laid out to dry. He screwed up his face to dramatize the importance of his next statement. "You can't just beg, you can't just whine, 'Please God, do this, please God, do that.' There's no power in that. But when you begin to *thank* God for what He's already doing in all His generosity, *then* the power begins to flow." He looked at me with those searching eyes and leaned back against the tree. He pulled a little rag from his pocket and carefully began to clean the outside of one of his shoes.

"That's why the Psalm says, 'The LORD inhabits the praises of His people.' When you begin to praise Him, and thank Him, the Lord is right there."

I leaned back against the tree, too, and looked out over the park. There were people all around, but you had to climb over a metal fence to get to this tree. I rarely took the time to sit with Whistling Jack, who was always there and always ready to talk. Even though cars were roaring past and people were shouting, it seemed quiet in this one spot. "I don't know, Whistling Jack," I said, as I pulled a bit of grass out of the ground. "I don't want to be one of those superficial people who say, 'Praise God. Thank You, Jesus,' all the time. It sounds so Pollyanna."

Whistling Jack stopped rubbing his shoe and looked at me. One eye was totally closed. "I'm not talking Pollyanna!" he roared. He looked up at the sky. "I'm not saying be like the guy who sees someone falling off the tenth floor. He sticks his head out the window on the fifth floor as the falling guy passes and says, 'Hey, so far so good!' I'm not talking about that kind of cheap, backslapping silliness. I'm talking about the kind of thankfulness that rises up in the darkest times like a mighty ocean." He put down the shoe and the rag and motioned with his big craggy hands, palms up, as if some immense reservoir of water were rising up from the depths of the earth right then.

"Look it up," Whistling Jack continued. He was warming up to the subject. "Look it up in John. When Jesus sees five thousand people plus, maybe twenty thousand people, all needing something to eat, all He's got is a little boy's lunch—five hamburger buns and two sardines. I know what most of us would be doing if we had such a monstrous need and such puny resources." Whistling Jack began to sneer. "We'd be whining, 'Please, God, get me out of this. I'm desperate. If You've ever helped me, help me now!' But look what Jesus prays. Go ahead, look it up."

I thumbed through a little New Testament and finally found it in John 6:11 NIV: "Jesus then took the loaves, gave thanks, and distributed to those who were seated as much as they wanted."

131

"You see what Jesus prays?" Whistling Jack was shouting again. I looked over at a mother on the sidewalk, who had started to lead her child farther away from the fence. "In the middle of all that horrible need, Jesus says, 'Thank You, Lord. Thank You for these five hamburger buns and these two sardines!' Wow! That is power!"

"You sound like my dad," I said. "He used to always tell me the story of an old woman in Oklahoma who had just two teeth, but she was so thankful. She was so thankful because one of the teeth was on her upper plate and one was on her lower plate, and when she bit down, the two teeth met!"

"That's it, brother, that's it!" Whistling Jack chuckled. He was beginning to make some connections now. "You see, once you begin to thank God, the power begins to flow through you, and you never know what might happen. You never know! It's like that ninety-nine-year-old woman. They asked her if she had any kids. She said, 'Not yet!'" He closed one eye and stared at me to see if I was listening. Whistling Jack picked up his shoe and his rag and began to clean the dust off the shoestring eyes. "Any day, you never know," he crooned. "This bed is not my cooling board, these walls are not my grave. Thank God, another day!" Whistling Jack sounded like a preacher. "You see, the power comes, when you finally realize that God always, always, always has one more solution than you have problems. You'd think that losing your son, like God did, would be the final tragedy. Nothing could be worse than that, it is so bad. But God made it good. That's why we call that day Good Friday. That's why there is no problem you encounter, no matter what it is, that God doesn't have a solution for, somewhere, somewhere down the line. When you thank God for that, the power comes. That's the key. Look, I've had some pretty shaky spots in my life and I refuse to be discouraged. A long time ago I cheated. I read the last page of the book, and guess what, we win."

Whistling Jack took plenty of time to talk. But he wasn't afraid to listen. "I learned about the power a long time ago in Hong Kong on a double-decker bus," I started. "I don't mind buses, but I hate crowded buses on hot days with no air conditioners. There were wall-to-wall people on this bus so that I was standing up and couldn't move. Even that wasn't so bad. What was bad was that the ceiling was six feet high and I'm six feet four. I had to bend my neck over on my shoulder like a chicken. After thirty minutes, I would roll my head over to the other side and wedge it between my shoulder and the ceiling. I felt the humidity and irritation rising in me. I loathed that bus and everyone in it.

"Then I thought, *Well, this is so terrible, at least I'm going to thank God in every single circumstance.* I prayed, *Dear God, it is so hot in here. So hot. But I thank You that You are the Light and there is no darkness in You, and this warm, warm day reminds me of Your light, and because of that, Your goodness!* Then I prayed, *Dear God, there's someone standing on my foot, but thank You God that I have a foot and* someday *I'll walk on it again.* Then I prayed, even stronger, *Dear God, there's someone coughing on my shoulder, but that reminds me that You are the true breath of life and provide breath for all living things no matter who we are!* My prayers started getting stronger and I started feeling better. Pretty soon that hot, crowded double-decker bus became a rolling tabernacle of praise all across the city for me. I stepped off feeling like a prince, refreshed, ready to praise my Lord."

Now I was the one speaking way too loud. Two teenagers stared at me from beyond the iron gate in spite of themselves. "That's it, brother, you've got it! Right in the middle of a hot day on a bus you found it. That's the key."

Whistling Jack put one of his huge paws on my shoulder. "You see, that's what I've come to believe. That is all faith is. People have so many fancy definitions for faith. But faith is nothing less than courtesy. It's courtesy. Let me give you an example. If you told me at this moment that you were going to go across the street and buy me a steak dinner and a huge cup of black coffee, what would I say right now? I'd say thank you. Even though I don't have it yet, I would say thank you because you're a friend. I trust you. Suppose I said, 'Yeah right. I'll believe it when I *see* it.' That would be so rude. I'd have been so discourteous. I bet you would never buy me a dinner again. So when God gives me a promise, and there's a heap of them in that Bible, I just thank Him, even though I haven't seen the result of some of them yet. I just say thank You because God is my friend and I trust Him."

"And even when God doesn't give you what you ask for, perhaps it's because He is giving you something else." I still felt talkative. "When Milton went blind—"

"Never heard of him," Whistling Jack said firmly.

"Well, when Milton went blind," I proceeded without paying any attention to him, "he wrote a poem. It was like, why did God take away the one thing he needed in order to serve Him—his sight? In the last lines of the poem, Milton realizes that God has all kinds of resources and servants. God doesn't need Milton. So Milton ends the poem by saying something like this—'He also serves who only stands and waits.'"

Whistling Jack had heard enough. "Your blind friend with that sissy name Milton sounds just like Paul. When Paul asks for the thorn in the flesh to be gone, God gives him something else— a revelation of how God's grace works through weakness."

Whistling Jack put his shoe down again and leaned toward me. "You see," he said, "here's the key that some guys never get." He pointed one of his huge fingers at me and paused for a moment. "God doesn't owe me nothing. Nothing. Everything I get is gravy. I just don't have a right to be resentful because I really didn't start with any cards I could trade off anyway! Not to God. I see this on the street all the time. The people that don't make it on the street are angry because they didn't get a square deal. They get angrier and angrier until they kill themselves or somebody else. It's crazy. The ones that make it find something to be thankful for in the worst of circumstances. I mean the worst! They are thankful, no matter how bad it gets, and you know what? They live."

I pulled some more grass out of the ground. "That's what my friends in Alcoholics Anonymous keep talking about. They keep saying the attitude of gratitude is not some optional religious thing that you can have if you want to. They say it is the key principle to survival. It is your life jacket. Without it you will drown in some gutter of resentment and vomit."

Whistling Jack cocked his head and rubbed his neck. The day was getting hotter, but the old tree and the green grass provided coolness. "Stop walking around inside my head. I was going to say what you just said," Whistling Jack growled. "As I see it, anyone who talks about being thankful ends up talking about contentment. That's what Paul said. I've learned that whatsoever state I am in, therewith to be content! It's so easy. If your needs are small, it doesn't take much to make you happy. People are always talking about whether the cup is half empty or half full. Maybe there's a third alternative. Maybe your glass is too big!" Whistling Jack was shouting again. "You see, if you had a smaller container, if your needs were smaller, you'd have a glass flowing over!" Whistling Jack looked at me sharply to see if I was getting it.

"I get it, I get it," I said. "You know, Socrates said something like that. He said that the richest man was the one who was content with the least."

Whistling Jack picked up his tattered hat and began to carefully pick the stray threads off it. "I don't know any Socrates," he intoned. "But I do know that once you're content, once you are thankful, you begin to treat others differently. That's the key."

I began to wonder how many keys there were, or if maybe they were all the same key. I just grunted and pulled on some more grass.

"It's like my brother used to tell me a long time ago." Whistling Jack's voice became more solemn and funeral. "If you don't like a man, walk a mile in his shoes. Then two things happen. One, you're now a whole mile away from him, and two, he's barefoot and you're wearing his shoes!" He checked me out with a questioning look and kept picking at his hat.

I paused for a while and let that last little bit of wisdom sink in. Whistling Jack put his hat down and leaned his head back

135

on the trunk and closed his eyes in what I can only assume was contentment. I said, "You know, in Dante's *Inferno*, the center of hell isn't hot, it's cold."

"I don't know about no Dante, now," Whistling Jack mumbled suspiciously, with his eyes still closed.

"Hell is ice cold," I continued. "It's a frozen lake, and Satan is frozen in it, and it's all upside down, like it's contrary to God's plan. And the lake stays frozen from the beating of Satan's wings. And he seems to be beating them in anger. He is gnashing his teeth, grinding up people, and I guess he's angry because the universe isn't the way he wants it. He just keeps chewing what Dante calls the 'eternal empty grudge.' That's the center of hell. That's the opposite of what you are talking about. Hell is being angry because things didn't turn out the way you want them to. Heaven is being thankful because God's personality shines through even in the worst of circumstances. This could be heaven right here in the middle of the Lower East Side, sitting under a black locust tree and looking up at the sky. In some ways, we're the richest men in the world. Isn't that right, Whistling Jack?"

Whistling Jack did not answer. His eyes were closed and his breathing was regular and heavy. I leaned my head back against the tree trunk, too, and looked up at the leaves. I thought of all the people in the park around me from the joyous three-year-old on the walk in front of me to the brooding old woman on the park bench across the courtyard. I thought of all the people in all the buildings surrounding the park and all the people in all the buildings behind them and on and on, extending out miles from sleeping Whistling Jack and from me.

I got up and decided to go across the street, to see if I could buy Whistling Jack a steak dinner and a huge cup of black coffee.

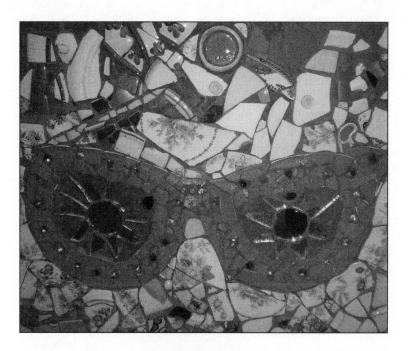

CHAPTER 20

Sight for
Sore Eyes

Be alert, stand firm in the faith, be brave, be strong.
1 CORINTHIANS 16:13 TEV

*To acquire knowledge, one must study; but to acquire
wisdom, one must observe.*
MARILYN VOS SAVANT

THE BIG CHURCH WAS FULL and there was no air conditioning. Members from many churches had gathered together to talk about our neighborhood and the city. A long-term church leader came up to the podium.

"Everybody like soup?" he shouted.

"Yeah," the group responded.

"I love to make good soup, don't you?"

"Yeah!" People were fanning themselves with paper, but they were with him.

"But to make a really good soup, you got to put in a lot of good ingredients. You don't just put celery in some water, and that's it. No way. You put a little chicken in the pot, some potatoes, a little corn, some sauce, and some carrots. Sometimes you let family and friends put something in, maybe some peppers and some onions. But what you want, for a really good soup, is a mix. And when all those things start cooking together, and you smell that aroma, it's wonderful, when you get a good mix, right?"

"Right!" echoed off the walls.

Everyone got quiet as the speaker took a long pause. "Now that's all we're saying as we talk to the developers and the city officials and the politicians when they come to talk to us about our neighborhood. We don't want just one kind of person in this neighborhood. We don't want just one culture, one economic group, one cluster of professionals, one kind of housing. When all the issues get complicated, we have one thing to say: Keep the mix!"

The group roared.

"Now," the leader was warming up, "when I was a little child in school, I couldn't see the blackboard. All I could see was some light fuzzy markings on the board. Nothing else. Finally my teacher said I needed to get some glasses, so I did. I remember two things after I got my glasses. First of all, I could see the writing on the blackboard! Every mark of the chalk was clear and sharp. I could read it. Second, I had a headache. It lasted all day. Somehow it hurt my head to see things so clearly."

The group was quiet again.

"Now, we've got to remember, that in order to see what is really happening, sometimes it hurts a little bit, and that's all right."

He sat down. An awkward silence was hanging over the room as people thought about the words. I left the building and walked back to our office. *It does hurt to see sometimes,* I thought, *and it hurts to see the changes.* I've seen so many good changes here in the city: Christ's resurrection power working in adults who were heading for destruction, children and youth taking a stand for the Lord, young adults going to college and getting a job instead of dealing drugs. I've seen teenagers of families who make money off drugs use their energy and intelligence to raise money for mission trips instead of for gold chains for their necks. Yet things are lost, too—the sense of family on the street, the sense of mutual protectiveness, the sense of working together to defend against outside danger.

As I walked, I thought about Whistling Jack's lack of interest in Dante. When Dante finally gets to heaven in *The Divine Comedy,* one of the things he emphasizes is how clearly he sees. Everything is sharp and bright, every leaf, every landscape. That's what heaven is all about. It's as if the curtains that veil our vision will finally be pulled back. It's as if we will finally get glasses. I felt a deep stirring just to see.

On our street I walked by a building our church is constructing and I looked at the shell. On one side of the building was a squat. Squatters often have very little and make do with primitive plumbing and electricity, or they make do with none at all. On the other side of the new building are brand-new luxury apartments. We, as the church, are in between. That is the present reality. I stood there and squinted my eyes, as if that would help me truly see what is happening. I have so many mixed feelings. There is so much good and so much loss.

I walked to the park and looked at it. The park is now like many parks in many cities. Homeless people lie on the benches. Some are just passing through for the day. Others are long-term street people who know everyone. Some are on public assistance and have little apartments in the area. But there are also professionals now in the park, reading their papers. Artists from middle-class families hang out in the park and pretend that they are somehow radical.

I entered the park and passed by Whistling Jack's tree. An evangelical group was doing a puppet show in the park now. These groups have also become part of the mix. The park has been flooded with them this year. They sing songs, do puppet shows, hand out water, or give out tracts. I help with some of these groups, and sometimes I see the wall of separation between the suburban visitor and the inner-city dweller come down. Walls crumble, miracles happen, people accept Christ.

Yet, to be honest, I see other Christian groups that miss the mark. I see the groups both from their own perspective, and perhaps a little bit from the perspective of someone who grew up in the neighborhood. Sometimes their style is so out of sync with the area it is like sending punk rockers to perform at a nursing home where the residents love the gentle melodies of Glenn Miller. The punk rockers may be totally sincere and well prepared as they diligently blast away, but they don't understand their audience.

Some groups in the parks come in for the day. At best people are touched by God's awesome grace. At worst, the groups are like tourists who come to a foreign country for a day but never take the time to learn the language. As I watched the children's puppet show, which also had a couple of skinheads and an older Polish man watching, I wanted to encourage the puppeteers to really look at their audience. "Don't just do something, stand there," I wanted to say.

As I watched the puppet show, a young man walked up to me who feels called by God to reach out to punks. He's just moved to the city, gotten a job and a place to stay in Manhattan. "It's worse than I thought here," the young man said. "Did you get my message about Chaos?"

How could I forget the two people my friend had been telling about for the last two weeks—Godshelter and Chaos. Their names have such poetry and heavy-handed symbolism. "No, I didn't get your message."

"Well, Chaos is dead. He died of a heroin overdose." I watched my young friend's face to see how he was handling his new environment. He was learning to see.

I walked to another part of the park and stood in a place where you used to be able to see the top of the Twin Towers. I thought about one of the Scripture verses I had taken for my own in this time of grief after September 11: "Rejoice with those who rejoice, weep with those who weep" (Rom. 12:15 NRSV). It's such a small verse, only six words in the original Greek. Several times I preached on the first phrase and several times I preached on the second. As I did so, I realized that both instructions are really saying the same thing—pay attention to the other person.

Pay attention to the other person—how easy to say. I stood in the corner of the park and knew I could point no fingers. I remember the stereotype of a Christian walking down a fancy hall on Sunday morning with a cheery personality, worn like a suit, and passing by someone with a hearty, "Hey, how you doing, brother?"

"I'm depressed and thinking about suicide."

"Hey, that's great, brother. God bless you!" he shouts over his shoulder as he walks in late to a Sunday school class where he's supposed to be speaking. I know I may not have been so obvious, but I've often done the same sort of thing.

In reality, no doubt much of what I do can be seen, at heart, to be a fancy way of saying, "Let's talk about you. What do you think of me?"

I looked up at the skyline and thought about all of the things I totally love about the city. The buildings that touch the stars, the birds that sing in snow, the little storefronts that give shelter, the trees that cool, the music that's free, even the sidewalks that provide firm steps. Yet there is something far more important. Sometimes when I am sharing Christ, I will look a person in the eye and say, "You are far more important than this entire city.

Because all the things in the city, this building, this neighborhood, the fancy cars, the money, all these things will pass away, but your soul will not. Cities will come and go, but your soul will continue forever." I want to pay attention, but I want to pay attention to the right thing. I couldn't get around it. For God, the right thing is the person. That is why a city, even an unattractive city, is so special. Even though I had said it earlier in my head, I had seen it later in my heart that people really are God's treasure. I was learning that this city must be a great treasure trove indeed, because a human being is very, very, precious. I squinted my eyes again and looked around.

I came to this city many years ago, first as a transient spectator. Then I came back and I wanted to do something for others. I wanted to be a doer, to help people both spiritually and physically. What had I really done? In all my doing, had I failed to see? Had I missed the mark, like those puppeteers performing a script for an old alcoholic who doesn't even speak English? Should I count my accomplishments on my fingers to prove to myself that I had really done something?

I stood there in the park a bit longer, feeling very blue. A tall sixteen-year-old came up and shook my hand. I had known Mark since he was a kid. I knew a bit about his family, which had a ton of troubles on their own. No one in his family went to church. Mark had been a troublemaker sometimes as a child and still had behavior problems when he went to our youth group. He was smart, obnoxious, bored, funny, violent, unpredictable, charming, abusive, and genuine. With all his talk, he seemed to care passionately about God. "Who gave birth to God?" he'd ask as a child. "Do you think there is life on other planets, and what has God done for them?" "Could I be a missionary?" His questions went on and on. I always liked him, although sometimes I was on guard, because I never knew when he might strike out at someone. But I always put myself in the role of the pastor, the one who baptized Mark, the one who was helping him, the one who prayed for him to grow up in the right way.

Last Sunday, during the invitation at our church, tall Mark loped down the aisle. I thought, "Well, Mark has come to rededicate his life. His commitment has been so erratic." I put my arm around him as people sang and asked him the question I had asked hundreds of times before: "Why did you come forward?" In my mind, I was preparing to pray a prayer of rededication and blessing for Mark.

But Mark said something that no one, young or old, had ever said to me before in that situation. "I came forward this morning to pray for you."

"OK," I mumbled. The people continued to sing the invitation song.

Mark put his arm around me, just like a pastor, and bowed his head. "Dear Lord," he said, "help Taylor to be a great pastor and bless him. Make things really good for him. Amen." Then Mark squeezed my shoulder and went back to his seat.

As I looked at Mark in the park I realized that maybe God hadn't even sent me here so that I could pray for the city. Maybe God had sent me here so that the people of the city could pray for me. Somehow the emotions of seeing how Mark had reached out for me crept up on me as I stood in the park. I walked with Mark silently to the corner.

"Thanks again," I croaked. That was all that would come out of my mouth, so I left him and lumbered back to the office.

CHAPTER 21

Re-Vision

*"Call to me and I will answer you, and will tell you
great and hidden things which you have not known."*
JEREMIAH 33:3 RSV

*In the turmoil of life without, and black despair within,
it is always possible to turn aside and wait on God. Just
as at the center of a hurricane there is stillness, and
above the clouds a clear sky, so it is possible to make a
little clearing in the jungle of our human will for a*

*rendezvous with God. He will always turn up, though in
what guise and in what circumstances cannot be fore-
seen—perhaps trailing clouds of glory, perhaps as a beggar, in the purity of the desert or in the squalor of
London's Soho or New York's Time Square.*

MALCOLM MUGGERIDGE

I WAKE UP EARLY ON A Saturday morning. It is a personal
anniversary of the heart. I am going back to Times Square to find
the flophouse I stayed in the first night I came to New York City,
nearly thirty years ago. I'm making the journey I write about in the
prologue. Here goes.

It only takes me a minute to put on my cargo pants, tennis
shoes, and T-shirt and take the dog out. A needle lies on the curb.
A hospital is on the corner, so perhaps the needle came from there.
It looks so medical—the orange cap over the point, the numbers on
the syringe.

But I know it wasn't used by a doctor. I stare at the needle as
I stand outside and hold my dog's leash. The morning air is cool
and misty. I have nothing to do but look.

This neighborhood has changed so much, yet I still see needles
outside the door when I walk the dog in the morning. My dog continues to root around and smell for things that I will never understand. I continue to stare at the needle. The needle reminds me that
when I sleep, deep in the night, people are doing unspeakable
things on my front stoop.

Catching someone shooting up on the street is always a con-
spiratorial moment. The bent body, the tourniquet on the arm, the
needle in the skin. It is as if you barged into someone's bathroom
or perhaps his bedroom. But the user will never look right at you.
The user has other interests.

I look around at the other items in the gutter—a dead mouse,
a cigarette butt, a deflated balloon, a broken beer bottle. The bottle's extending fragment looks like the tooth of some dangerous

predator. I think about all the other things that happened in front of my building as I slept. I look up. I used to be able to see the Twin Towers from here.

My dog has done her business. I leave her at the apartment and head out for the thirty-block walk to Times Square, to find whatever memories can uncover.

The noise of the garbage truck blankets the street. A man pushes a laundry cart up the block, looking for bottles. Starlings twitter and fight in the air. Down the street, the engine of a huge crane tells me the rebuilding project has begun on the office building.

This is not some practical errand. This is my private prayer walk, a personal pilgrimage. I am happy. I feel like one of the singers in Psalms, who turned to his city and sang, "'All my fountains are in you'" (Ps. 87:7 NIV).

As I turn the corner, the spire of the Chrysler Building stands in the distance, catching the morning sun. The sun also plays with the trees in the park. The six-sided stones on the sidewalk fit so neatly together, a counterpoint to the messiness of our human lives. Three men sleep on the sidewalk in cardboard boxes under an American flag.

I am as excited as a hiker starting out on the Appalachian Trail. The leaves of the street trees rustle above me; the dull grind of the air conditioners provides background music. The smells of bread and hot coffee in the bakery catch my interest. The fragrances of cheese from the deli, flowers from the florist, onions from the market draw me along. Every sign above every storefront is sharp and clear. I feel like a pioneer, seeing the undiscovered land anew, a visitor from another world, drinking in every color and texture for the first time. It is an uncharted wilderness, with a new astonishment around every corner and across every street. Now I am not only smelling the possibility of a thousand adventures, I am journeying back to my own first glimpse of the city. Speak, memory.

As I walk up Broadway, I look up, and I see what I have learned to take the time to see—gargoyles, towers, decorative edges, gardens, circular windows, ornamental clocks all at the top of the buildings around me. Down below on the sidewalk, this part of Broadway is empty. It is ruled at this time of day by a few thin, soiled men who sleep on the street, wandering around now looking for pocket change to get a cup of coffee. A few store owners are unlocking window gates; others are sweeping the sidewalks. The contrast to what this part of Broadway will look like later makes it feel as quiet and solitary as a cathedral.

One man wanders back and forth on the sidewalk, talking to himself or to some invisible friend. His clothes are dingy and his shoes untied. He has a greasy backpack with a shopping bag hanging from the back. "I got it down, I got it down, I got it down. Don't beat me, don't beat me, don't beat me. Don't listen to the soldiers, don't listen to the soldiers, don't listen to the soldiers," he continues in a measured monotone. Off to the side of Broadway looms the Empire State Building. Because of the sun, the east side of the building is a solid silver-white shaft of burning light, reflecting the hopes of the morning like the blade of a sword.

The view from Broadway shows a cluster of buildings up ahead close to Times Square. From here the buildings look like castles, packed together, some towers in the shade, some towers catching the morning light. Strength surges into my legs with every step. The sidewalk is swallowed by my purposeful stride now.

What you love you learn about. God is love, and on this pilgrimage, a great love for the forgotten people of the city pierces my heart anew. It is a love not only for the people, but for the whole city, the storefronts, trees, pets, cars, sidewalks, locks, bars, buses, billboards—the whole buzzing, swarming place. My home.

Larger billboards tower over me as Times Square gets closer. As Habakkuk said, they are signs so large that a person could see them as they run (Hab. 2:2). Sleepy-eyed tourists amble around in this area. They look like I did thirty years ago, a little stunned, a little wary, a little wide-eyed with the infinite possibilities.

Times Square. The huge multiple screens, displaying jokes, showing models, giving headlines. The walls of the buildings themselves are now in motion, spinning and writhing with colors, pictures, and messages.

I walk toward Port Authority, the bus station where I first arrived. I'm remembering what it felt like so many years before. There were a lot more peep shows and porn shops and triple-X signs for the adults then. There seem to be more tourists now, with colorful, unwrinkled clothing and nice teeth. Still, here is a woman, dirty and tired, hungry for drugs, walking slowly along the side of the buildings, looking for something, a potential customer or a friend. I step over a pile of vomit next to the curb. As I walk, I begin to feel I am nineteen years old again, with all the same amazement and questions.

The bus station has been remodeled. The P.A. system now soothes us with classical music. The rest rooms seem safer, with a little less of the nightmarish edge. Still a man outside the rest rooms shouts at three policemen surrounding him. "Leave me alone! Leave me alone! Get out of my face!" he screams, as they move closer. Another policeman comes up to me as I stand by, looking on. "Please move on," he says, firmly. I am a kid again, told what to do as I first arrive. I drift into the river of people passing by as I did so many years ago. The same bubbling stew of possibilities surround me.

In the river of people outside the bus station, one man catches my eye. He is dirty, with tousled hair that looks as though he has just gotten up. Yet his face is both intent and fierce. He is leaning on the armrests of a wheelchair and pushing it backward. He has only one leg, but he is pushing that wheelchair fast. Every hop has such an athletic focus. I try to follow him but cannot catch up with him because of all the people bumping me. A wave of compassion sweeps over me. This young man was not even alive when I first came here at nineteen, eager-eyed and self-absorbed. I had two legs, but on the inside, I was hopping along just as fast and furiously as I could, looking for I don't know what. What is this man pressing for with all his might? A buck? A cigarette? An answer? I know now something I hadn't even considered at nineteen—that this one man's hopes and fears weighed more in the balance than all the Chrysler Buildings, billboard signs, and stores in the city. His little strivings may be forgotten by the transportation experts and financial planners, but he is not forgotten. I try to see where the man and the wheelchair go, but he is walking too fast.

I drift with the flow of people uptown and turn off on a side street. Is this the street where the flophouse was? Is this the place where I turned off, eyes as big as frying pans? I can't quite remember. Was the building torn down? Is this the right block? I no longer feel purposeful and sure.

A verse comes to me: "Call to me and I will answer you, and will tell you great and hidden things that which you have not known" (Jer. 33:3 NRSV). For the first time in many years, I remember my second-grade teacher. I would sit at my little desk, trying to understand some vastly complex addition or subtraction problem. "A boy with two apples went three miles . . ." it might begin. I would look and look at the math problem, but I couldn't determine what the right answer was. I couldn't figure it out. Finally, I would go up to the teacher's huge oak desk, as big as a boat, and wait in line to ask her a question. Here's the strange part—when my turn came, I would put my math book on her desk and start to ask my question. Then, even though I had read the problem twenty times, as I stood next to the teacher, I would see the answer. She wouldn't have said a word. The same words were there as before, but now there was a solution. "Oh, I see it," I'd say, and return to my desk. Now, somehow, on this hot street, I feel like a second-grader, simply wanting to stand by my Teacher.

Dear, Lord, I pray as I walk, *I've seen so many signs and huge billboards and video screens today that mean nothing. Show me some sign from You. I remember the sign right here on this street: "Rooms—$10 a night." It helped me find a safe place to stay so long ago, when I was on the run from You.*

Perhaps this is the row of buildings where I was. "No Loitering" the door says in large letters. "Stronger Rent Laws Now" is taped to the wall. In the window is a small faded photocopy of the Statue of Liberty, with no other explanation. A metal sign is posted officially on the door frame: "No Trespassing—This Building Is for Tenants and Their Guests Only—Manhattan DA's Trespass Program." No sign here for me. I walk a few more steps, feeling sadder and sadder. Was there just an endless stream of instructions and advertisements with no meaning? Wait a minute. Was there a theater here before, where I slept with the lock blown off the door? I look on one side of the door in hopes there is a sign for me. The sign says *The Vagina Monologues*. The letters on the sign are large and catchy but not much else. I look down and sigh. The sun is beating down on my shoulders. My eyes begin to focus on a stone closer to the sidewalk. What's this faded bit of lettering down in the corner, etched in the brownstone? On one side of the little inscription, it says 1855. On the other side, I think it says 1880, although part of the last number is knocked out. In between the two dates are three small words: *Christus der Eckstein*. I bend over, place my fingers on the small letters, and try to remember. "Christ the cornerstone," in German. Memories rush in from the place where I was headed the first time I was here: Berlin. I don't really need to know the historical details of this inscription. For me, it is a reminder in code from other newcomers to New York from another time. I have no idea what their story was, but I realize that they, too, were immigrants to the city, just as I am. I look up to the sunshine and take a deep breath. The three words are enough for me. Hidden in all the glaring spectacular contrasts of the city is still the foundation of Christ, the cornerstone. The words in stone were there the first time I had been on this street at nineteen years old, looking for an answer to my problems. I just hadn't noticed. But Christ's long-term purpose of self-giving love was there then and is still here now.

A story comes back to me that I heard about an inner-city worker in Trenton, New Jersey. He had just told the story of Noah's ark to a small group of inner-city boys in the mission church. After telling them about the rainbow, he asked this question: "Where do

you look to see God's promise?" He wanted them to say that we look up in the sky.

"You look down," one boy said solemnly.

They weren't getting it. "No, where do you look to see the sign of God's promise?" This time, he pointed with his finger to the sky to encourage the right answer.

"You look down," the little boy said again.

A third time the worker asked the question, and for a third time the boy was adamant. Finally, the worker stopped, looked at the boy, and tried to understand. He tried to see things from the boy's perspective. Where the boy lived, because of the buildings, there wasn't a lot of sky visible, and the boy had never seen a rainbow there. But he *had* seen a rainbow as he looked down on the street, in a mud puddle with a little bit of car oil in it. The rainbow there was crystal clear for him to see.

God's promise is always in the city. We just have to learn how to see it.

Ending: Jesus

They will see his face.

REVELATION 22:4A NIV

You become what you look at.

WHISTLING JACK
REVELATION 21–22

IN THE LAST PAGES OF THE BOOK, He Himself comes to live in the city. He loves the city so much, He's married to it. The city is so beautiful to Him that it's like His bride. He will live with His people. For Him, they are the city.

There are no more money problems. People can drink the water of life for free. The street plan of the city is indescribably beautiful. The entries to the city never close. The boundaries and structures of the city are unspeakably vast.

In this city, there are no more tears, no more curses, no more darkness, no more temple, no more barriers between us and Him.

But there in the center are the primal, primary things: the river, the tree, the leaves, the street. The Bible makes sure we know the street will be there. The nations will be healed. In some unutterable way, many of the things I see in the city now will be there, but they will all be new. The homeless will have a home; the street people will be remembered.

People's sight will no longer be darkened or dimmed. No one will need a streetlight or even the sun. God will be the light. We will finally truly see that face, that face we previously glimpsed only in faint outline.

In the whole vast drama of the Bible, it seems as though coming to His city is the last thing Jesus does.

But not really.

Epilogue

OK, SO I NEVER FOUND THE FLOPHOUSE. If you've read this far, you know that. If you cheated and read the prologue and now you're hunting through the epilogue for the answer, well, you found it. Whistling Jack always told me, though, that the point of surfing (as if he knew anything about the point of surfing) is not to get to the beach. It's the ride. And loving the city is a ride.

In the prayer at the beginning of the book, I ask if there is pleasure in seeing a parking lot. With a little child as a guide, instructing us to look down at the gorgeous colors in an oil slick, I have my answer. Yes, there is pleasure in looking. Looking is part of the ride.

I'm asking four friends from our mission to help me in closing. Each of them is very dear to me. I chose them because each has helped me see the city differently. I'd love to have included a hundred others. The cultural diversity of the group is incidental. To have the testimony of four people—one of African-American descent, one of Puerto Rican descent, one of Chinese descent, and one of Yugoslavian descent—might have been planned in the twentieth century. Now, in a twenty-first-century city church, such diversity is simply assumed. Through Christ, the walls between people are crumbling. I asked these people to share a bit of their own experiences and how Christ had helped them see the city differently.

Testimony: Matthew

Grace in a Crack House

I was lying in the back of a crack house when I began to come to myself.

How do I describe what it is like to be on the streets? Complete hopelessness. It is wandering from neighborhood to neighborhood, glaring at everything and everyone. I was filling myself with hate and the desire to harm everyone around me.

I was bouncing back and forth between anger and hopelessness as though I were on a Ping-Pong table.

I came to see in the strangest of places—lying in the back room of a crack house. It was someone's apartment, with people coming and going and using a variety of drugs. As a teenager, if I saw a dope addict, I considered him a piece of garbage. I could never see myself as part of his world. Addicts were like Martians. Once I entered that world of drugs and homelessness, it was so different than I expected.

I have no doubt that there is a lot of blatant ruthlessness and inhumanity in that world. That's obvious. Yet my experience was different. In my worst times, I entered a world in which people get through life's wounds with alcohol and drugs. In the crack house I would go to, I was welcome with or without money.

As I lived in that world, I began to see the humanity of each person that drugs cannot push out. It may seem like blasphemy to say this, but all of those people doing drugs in that place were really calling on the Lord.

"Have you seen Joe?" they'd say. "He looks good. He's clean. They say he's in a program. I need to get in a program. I know what I'm doing is not right."

Then before they'd take that hit or that drink or that blast, they'd say, "God forgive me. I wish I didn't need this."

Then, there in that apartment, people would often drift into a circle, almost as if they were in a program, and begin to share their pains and disappointments. For a time, I tried to put on a show. It was a game that nobody could play. People genuinely could feel my pain. I could tell.

Through all this, somehow God was speaking to me, strange as that sounds. God was saying, "What do you have in common with these people?" We all had an understanding that this was not what God wants for us. There was a truth building up through the "coulda-shoulda-woulda" attitude. I began to see the humanity fighting through the drug mentality all around me. Through those darkest days, something would not let me *not* have a Bible with me. I was reading Scriptures there in the back bedroom of the crack house. I remembered my partner in the military service in Korea who told me "Christ will never leave you." I remembered accepting Christ as Lord with him in a Bible study in the barracks long ago.

Somehow, thinking about these things and reading the Bible in the middle of all the drug use, Christ began to lift me up. I started walking and took the step to a special program to help me. I found strength and began working so I would not wallow in my own vomit. Christ lifted me up. Now I am with Christ and God is with me, allowing Christ to grow in me.

Because of Christ, I see people differently now. He now helps me identify and empathize and commiserate with others. He also allows me to get angry with those for continuing to batter and abuse themselves. God, in His sense of humor, has now given me a chance to work in shelters and rehabilitation programs. God has done a creation act in me. He has created the ability for me to see the grace and the victory in the lives of others who have gone through the same things I've gone through. He has given me joy out of being allowed to pay back the grace I've seen and be an extension of Him. Working with the people I do helps me never get out of the battle of being human and helps me never get disconnected from reality again.

Not long ago, I was at a shelter, leading a group. I heard a voice shout, "Matthew, Matthew! Oh my goodness! I know him! I know him! I know him!"

I looked over and saw a woman I knew. Her place was one of the crack houses I frequented when I was doing badly. She was beside herself. She was so genuinely glad that I was doing well and that I was clean, healthy, and positive.

Seeing her with the eyes of Christ did something to me too. I didn't see just a dirty, homeless woman at the end of her rope, fighting for whatever she could get. I saw something else because of Christ. I saw a human being, reaching out through all the drugs, heartache, and violence to make a real connection with me.

Matthew Williams
Member at Graffiti

Testimony: Marisel

The Mirror

I was high. I was into drugs. I spent a lot of time smoking marijuana, drinking beer, and hanging out on the streets. I was in the clubs and bars and I was neglecting my family. I was in anyplace a human being could be, a place you could think of that was not appropriate for my kids.

I had times when I felt this life wasn't right for me. Sometimes I got so high I didn't dare go upstairs and show my face to my children.

At that time my oldest daughter embarrassed me. She had given her heart to Jesus. When I came up to the apartment, she was very quiet. She told me to look at myself. She said, "Go look at yourself in the mirror." I remember it well, how she stood behind me as I looked into that mirror and saw what drugs, drinking, and my lifestyle were doing to me.

It was disgusting. I remember really looking and seeing how skinny I was. There were big dark places under my eyes. My hair was messed up and my clothes were ragged. I looked as though I had AIDS. I was so embarrassed I started crying.

My daughter stood behind me. "You can do better than that," she said quietly. Somehow, with the mirror and my daughter behind me, I began to see. In one sense, I had to face that I was just a drunk, just a piece of garbage.

So that Sunday, December 19, I walked into the church. I felt I didn't belong there. I thought I was the most evil thing in the world. I felt so dirty. But that day, I listened to the music, I talked to the people. They were so nice to me. I talked to the pastor that day. He drew some pictures to show me exactly what it meant to ask Christ into my life. I prayed and asked for forgiveness of my sins and made Christ my Lord right then.

I started feeling very, very clean. I can't describe it. I went back to the street and saw everything differently. I saw people hanging out on the street and doing drugs. At first a wave of anger went over me. I wanted to shout, "Don't do that. That's not good for you." Then I began to feel sorry for them. Now, sometimes I stand by them and tell them about God. I tell them my own story, how I accepted Christ and left heavy drugs overnight.

Now I take care of myself. I feel happy, and I never felt that before. Before I hated everybody. And now, stronger than ever, I can't see anybody sick. I feel I need to be a doctor with compassion and another kind of healing. I'll take care of anybody now. Everything, everything in my neighborhood looks so different, since I stopped and looked in that mirror.

Marisel Lugo
Member at Graffiti

Testimony: Uros

The Shell Game

I grew up in a rough part of Belgrade. The upper part of the area was very wealthy, but where I lived was totally poor. We saw how well the children were treated in the upper part, but it was a totally different world from where we lived. There was a huge social contrast between these two worlds. We were not welcome in the upper world.

Even as a child, I lived in a neighborhood full of prostitution, drugs, and violence. People were always trying to show how strong they were. I would practice how to punch every day, because there were fights all the time. You were always trying to fight someone bigger than you were, in order to show how tough you were. Young children would carry guns, and they would shoot someone just to show they had "heart."

I was arrested many times. The first time, I was eleven years old; I had stolen a car. Eventually the authorities wanted to put me in a special institution because I had no respect for authority at all.

Our neighborhood was called "the home of the Game." We were famous for what you would call the shell game. We would work in a team and set up a box somewhere. We would plant several people in the crowd as "customers." They were supposed to guess which box the match was under. The one moving the boxes around knew how to trick the onlookers. Other people in the team would stand on the outskirts and look for police. I would sometimes be one who watched for police. It was a classic setup. I suppose it happens in cities all over the world. The planted customers in the crowd

160

would make a bet, and several of them, through time, would win. From the outside, it looked as though people were winning money.

Some person from the country would come into the city for the first time, and he never realized what was happening. If he would not make a bet himself, one of our team, who was acting like a customer, would ask the out-of-towner to join him in a bet. We would laugh at the people who were such suckers.

Everything in our neighborhood was like that shell game. We would wake up in the morning full of fear, look around, and see who we could mess up that day. We would easily lie and cheat to get what we wanted.

My parents were beautiful people. There was nothing wrong with them. They didn't understand why I developed the way I did. They had to work all the time, so I was out on the street on my own a lot. When they came home, they were very tired and had a lot of bills to pay. They worked hard for me, but in a sense, as I look back from my perspective now, they were worshiping idols too. If you're not with God, you're on your own. You don't have to be in my neighborhood to see this happening. You can see it if you look anywhere in the world.

I came to the Lord through what I call a vision. The Lord showed me the way. *Vision* may not be the best word to use. It was not like in the movies, in which some kind of vision is shown on the screen. I've never read or seen anything like it. I didn't see pictures before my eyes. But somehow I knew what to do. I realized I was supposed to be a servant of God. There was no question about it.

I received the gift of music. I was specifically called to do jazz music for the Lord. I didn't understand it at the time. There was no jazz music or jazz for the Lord in my area. I received an understanding of the laws of music. It was wonderful.

After that, I talked about Jesus to everyone. They thought I was totally crazy. Some thought I had flipped out on drugs. One day, in a store, I met one of my friends I had known a long time. A long time before, he was a nice kid, and I introduced him to all the

161

bad things on the streets. He had become one of the worst criminals in the city. His picture was in the newspapers sometimes.

He wanted to know what happened to me. I went back to his apartment to talk. Somehow, with this terrible criminal, I opened the Bible. As we read, the Lord talked to us. We read the passage that says the sheep know the voice of the Shepherd. I said to him, "Man, I know this voice!" Instantly, I knew it was the voice of Jesus.

My friend, this criminal, said, "You know what, I know that voice too." My friend accepted the Lord and was born again.

Later, I baptized him in a river in Belgrade, along with another friend. The Holy Spirit is so good. I became a jazz musician for the Lord. My friend became a playwright, and another friend became a painter. God is working to help us do something beautiful for Him.

My view of the world and my neighborhood changed after I accepted Jesus. I saw that so much of what I had done was fake. I had been full of fear. Everyone was lying and deceiving others. I saw that, really, I had grown up in hell. Everything was a shell game, and I was hustling to take advantage of others so that I wouldn't be taken advantage of.

As I grew in Christ, I began to see that the same pattern, the shell game, was operative in many aspects of human experience. I saw it in the government, politics, entertainment, music, and even in some churches. I saw that the shell game, with its manipulation and greed, was a part of many of the systems of the world.

But now that I am born again, I am a part of a different world. Instead of thinking how I can mess someone up, I am thinking about how I can lead someone to Christ. In Christ, I live in a light that was so different from the darkness of that fake and lying world. Instead of fear, I have faith, as a precious gift from God. After the Lord came to me, I felt as though I had awakened from a long sleep.

Uros Markovic
Musician at Graffiti

Testimony: Tim

The Man with One Leg

I am a loan officer working right next to where the World Trade Center stood. I remember coming out of the subway on September 11 and seeing a beautiful clear sky. I also remember seeing the smoke.

I stood there and watched. I was like a spectator. I probably should have left then. But I stayed simply to see what was happening. When the plane hit the second tower, there was a huge fireball. I felt the impact all over. Glass and debris started falling down on me and the other people in the street.

I just turned my head and saw people running everywhere. Then I saw an older lady fall. Another man and I went back to pick her up, and we simply said, "Come on now, it's time to go." At that time I felt calm but a little confused about everything.

The police said there could be more planes coming. I ran up the block toward city hall. All the firefighters and police were rushing toward the towers. I found a quiet little space close to city hall, where no one was, and I just prayed. I prayed that God would give those officers strength.

Then when the tower fell, all of Lower Manhattan started running. Things were falling all around, and I was thinking, *Oh no, this can't be happening.* It was like a volcano when all the ashes start coming down. You know the debris is going to hit you, and there's nothing you can do about it. I picked up my pace a bit as I moved away from the collapse, but I knew the smoke and debris were going to reach me. I was going through an underpass leading to Chinatown. That's where there was a woman screaming. She didn't know what to do. We were at an embankment where she was going to have to jump eight or ten feet. She didn't want to. A man next to me and I both told her, "Go ahead and jump! We'll catch you!" The debris by this time had completely overtaken us. Our eyes were burning. We could hardly breathe. It smelled kind of like tires burning. It wasn't the smoke so much as all the ashes everywhere.

"I can't get down!" the woman kept screaming. "What am I going to do?" She sounded hysterical.

We kept shouting, "Go ahead and jump!" Finally, she jumped and we caught her. We helped her go her own way.

But then an incident happened in all that debris and chaos that affected me more than anything else. I approached a man who had one leg. The debris was already over us. The smoke was everywhere. I remember vividly seeing this silhouette of a man with two crutches and one leg. He was an older man, and he wasn't very well dressed. He might have been homeless. As everybody was rushing frantically around him, he kept moving on his way as if he were going about his everyday business. He was probably the last person in the area. Everyone else at that time was running. I went over to him and said, "Can I help you? Can I carry you? I don't want to leave you behind." It's strange how just a few words could have such an impact on me. He simply said, very calmly, "No, I got it. I'm fine." I can't explain it, but I felt so much more calm after that.

I remember going through the tunnel and reaching Chinatown. I knew then we were in a little bit safer situation. I remember simply seeing him walking ahead of me. Somehow seeing the man with one leg making it gave me a deep sense of peace.

Then I had strength enough to continue. I saw an older lady who had almost collapsed. She seemed delirious, in a daze. I grabbed her arm and said, "Please, lady, come on." In a calm voice, I started talking to her about God. "God wants you to make it. Do you have children? Well, God wants you to see your children."

Finally, her feet started moving again. "I know you're going to make it," I said. "This is not our time yet; let's go." In some way, because of the encouragement I received from the man with one leg, I felt I had a small part in helping this delirious woman get away.

I came to know Christ as a teenager, but I feel that my experience on September 11 helped me to see the city more through Christ's eyes. I can't explain it. I really don't think the city has changed, but my view of the people is different. There is a lot of pressure at my job, but I see the beauty in people more. I'm not as quick to say someone is wrong. Personally, I feel more humbled.

I won't deny that it was tough for me to go back to Ground Zero. It was tough walking past the site each day, smelling the burning smell, seeing the thousands of notes and tributes put up. I know people need closure, but sometimes it was hard for me to see people from all over come to the construction site, people who hadn't been there on September 11. It was hard for me to see the magazines and photos that were sold, that money was being made off the event. I still don't quite understand all that. I had gotten married in a previous year on September 11, and so I have all kinds of emotions about that date. I still flinch when I hear planes overhead. I still see in my mind's eye the clear sky and that first glimpse of smoke as I came out of the subway. Death was everywhere that day, and I saw people die. For me it was horrible to see how long it took the falling people to hit the ground. People were so afraid where I was standing.

I suppose as I walk the streets of the city, I have a much deeper sense of gratitude. That man with one leg will never know how much his calmness and determination helped me that day.

I know that things can change any moment, for good or for bad. I know more deeply now that the key is having a living relationship with Christ, in both the good and the bad. Everything can change in a moment, as September 11 proved to me personally. No matter what happens, I know the circumstances of this world cannot take away my identity.

As a Christian, my personal story of that day involves what I and my coworker did afterward. We started a small Bible study at work. My coworker says he would have never started meeting except for the tragedy. I think we would have started the group but probably later. In my studies with my coworker, I'm learning what to pray for. God doesn't want us to suffer. But things happen for a reason we may not understand. That realization does not necessarily make things more difficult. In fact, for me personally, that realization is deeply satisfying because on a basic level I can now more truly trust in God. After September 11, I see my circumstances and the people around me so very differently. For that, I am grateful.

Tim Chin
Member at Graffiti

Note to Searchers

CHRIST DOES HELP US TO SEE, just as He did for the preceding four people who told you a little part of their stories. But, first of all, Christ pulls us out of the dark hole we have dug for ourselves. He saves us.

Perhaps Christ has been working in your life in recent times, but you are unsure about what is happening. There is no better time to be sure than right now. God wants you to know that you have eternal life (1 John 5:13). Turn to Him now to make sure.

The way to do so is simple. Agree with God concerning the things you have done wrong. God promises through Christ to clean you of every sin (1 John 1:9). As you talk to God, God's Spirit might bring to mind things you have done that you know were not right in His eyes. Whatever sin comes to mind, simply recognize it and rest in God's promise to forgive you.

Now, welcome our living Lord, Jesus, into your life. It is as if Christ were knocking at the door of your life, and you opened the door and said, "Come in." When you ask Christ into your life, He promises to come in (Rev. 3:20).

Once you have asked Jesus into your life, you simply trust Him. You rest in the promise that He made to come into your life. "Trust" and "believe" and "have faith" are all the same word in the Bible. It is the way we were designed to live. God has promised a new life in Christ. Trust simply means ceasing from the abnormal yet persistent habit of considering God a liar. We can rest in the way we were meant to live (John 3:16).

Now that you have welcomed Christ into your life through trust, your existence does not consist of merely keeping a lot of rules and regulations. As you rest in God's promises, you are able to allow Christ to work through you. There are some specific things that will help you in this new life. For example, get a Bible of your own and write in the back that you asked for forgiveness and welcomed Christ into your life. Write it in your own words, sign it, and date it. If you ever doubt that you asked Christ in, turn to that page to remind yourself. Since Christ promised to come in, your new life of trust means you only have to ask Him once. Reading parts of the Bible every day protects you from doubt.

Within twenty-four hours of this time, it is good to tell someone what you have done. It may be someone you know is a Christian or it may be someone close to you. For some reason, doing this will strengthen your own trust in God.

Find a Bible-believing church to go to the first week. Either ask a Christian you know for a recommendation or look around your neighborhood, or even look in the Yellow Pages. It needs to be a church that clearly depends on God's Word. The church people will help you in the next steps.

Finally, get ready to see in new ways. As the missionary at the beginning of the book said, you will find that receiving Christ feels as though you were cured of being color-blind.

Notes

1. Elie Wiesel, *The Gates of the Forest*, quoted by Larry Crabb, *The Silence of Adam* (Grand Rapids, Mich.: Zondervan, 1995), 19.

2. Francis Schaeffer, quoted by Taylor Field, *Peace in a Violent World* (Birmingham, Ala.: Women's Missionary Union, 1998), 5.

3. Rudolph Flesch, ed., *The Book of Unusual Quotations* (New York: Harper & Brothers, 1957), 48.

4. Desiderius Erasmus, introduction to the Greek New Testament, 1516–35.

5. Leonard Shlain, *Art and Physics* (New York: Quill, 1991), 364.

6. Ralph Waldo Emerson, *Basic Selections from Emerson* (New York: New American Library, 1954), 17.

7. Anthony C. Meisel and M. L. Del Mastro, trans., *The Rule of St. Benedict* (New York: Image Books, 1975), 89.

8. Brother Lawrence, *The Practice of the Presence of God* (Springdale, Pa.: Whitaker House, 1982), 7.

9. Ernest Hemingway, *A Farewell to Arms* (New York: Scribner's, 1929), 239.

10. Paul Davies, *God and the New Physics* (New York: Simon and Schuster, 1983), 128.

11. Aleksandr Solzhenitsyn, "A World Split Apart," *Finding God at Harvard: Spiritual Journeys of Christian Thinkers*, Kelly Morris, ed. (Grand Rapids, Mich.: Zondervan, 1996), 48.

12. Blaise Pascal, *Pascal's Pensees* (New York: E. P. Dutton, 1958), section 3, 52–70.

13. Bill Clinton, graduation speech to Stuyvesant High School, New York City, 6 June 2002.

14. Aldous Huxley, quoted in church meeting, New York, date and speaker unknown.

15. Albert Schweitzer, quoted in unpublished article, "The Greatest Moustache of the Twentieth Century," by Taylor Field, 2002.

16. Joanna Weaver, *Having a Mary Heart in a Martha World* (Colorado Springs, Colo.: WaterBrook, 2000), 9.

17. Desiderius Erasmus, *The Encyclopedia of Religious Quotations*, Frank S. Meade, ed. (Westwood, N. J.: Fleming H. Revell, 1965), 52.

18. E. B. White, *Here in New York* (New York: Warner Books, 1949), 52–53.

19. Ibid., 55.

20. Abraham Joshua Heschel, *I Asked for Wonder: A Spiritual Anthology*, Samuel H. Dresner, ed. (New York: Crossroad, 1983), 94.

21. Ibid., 95.

22. Ibid., 89.

23. Ron Mehl, *The Tender Commandments* (Sisters, Ore.: Multnomah, 1988).